Elvis,
the Blind Man,
and
the Man with the Tattoos

Elvis,
the Blind Man,
and
the Man with the Tattoos

Monica Vivian

To order additional copies of this book, contact:
Xlibris Corporation
1-888-795-4274
www.Xlibris.com
Orders@Xlibris.com
52311

Contents

You may recognize the settings of these stories because these stories are true. To maintain the privacy of those involved, identifying characteristics have been altered.

Special thanks to Mrs. Massachusetts, Pilar, and St. Nancy the Junior (you know who you are). Your unwavering support is truly appreciated and will not be forgotten.

4Alex2

All in the Name of Elvis

I knew Molly was in trouble when she called me up and asked me if I thought she was spending too much of her time focusing on Elvis. Knowing how to stifle a conversation, I quickly told her that indeed I did think she was focusing too much energy on a dead person, and the fact that she was battling with this question was telling in itself. Mind you, it was not my intention to immediately terminate this phone call, but Molly had other designs. "Oh, so you believe Elvis is dead," Molly said.

"Yes," I replied, "don't you remember? We were together the day he died."

Molly's family owned a day care center in the small town that we lived in during the 1970s. She was working there temporarily while she deliberated over her life's direction. I was completing an internship during the summer, something to show that I had experience working with children. I was attending the university, working toward a teaching degree, and wanted as much experience as possible. It was the summer of 1977. The year that Elvis died. We were both at the day care center when the news arrived. No children had reported that day, so work was slow. Molly was listening to the radio in the business office while I played cards with her eighteen-year-old brother, who lived in the basement.

Our game was interrupted by screams from Molly, "No, no! It can't be true!" We threw our cards down and rushed into the business office. Tears were streaming down Molly's face, her shoulders heaving as she sobbed.

She looked up at us and through gasps murmured, "Elvis . . . I . . . dead . . ."

"What?" I asked.

"Elvis is dead!" she yelled at me.

Startled by her response, I took a step back. "Elvis is dead?" I responded.

"Yes, Elvis is dead!" she yelled at me again.

"What happened?" I asked, still puzzled by her response.

"He died!" she spat.

"Oh," was all I could muster. I looked at her brother, who rolled his eyes and left the room. "I'm sorry," I said.

Molly did not respond but continued to cry. I put my arm around her shoulder and handed her a tissue. I didn't know what else to do. We sat like this for about fifteen minutes when suddenly Molly announced that she was closing the center for the day in memory of Elvis. She needed to go home and think. I called my sister and asked her to pick me up. She agreed and was startled when she saw Molly standing at the top of the stairs.

"What's up with her?" she asked.

"She's upset about Elvis," I said.

"Elvis?" my sister asked.

"Yes," I said, "Elvis died today."

"Oh, I didn't hear anything about it," my sister stated.

I looked at Molly standing at the top of the stairs in her own despair. She didn't see me wave goodbye—she just stood and stared. "I hope she's OK," I said.

That was twenty-five years ago. Today, I had Molly on the phone, and she still had not let go of Elvis. "Well, some of us believe that Elvis is still alive," she said curtly and hung up the phone. Over the course of time, Molly had somehow developed a belief that Elvis's death had been staged, and that Elvis had really fled to Mexico because the Mafia was after him. I never really understood how the Mafia was involved, but I accepted this as being Molly's reality. According to Molly, Elvis had hired a double to impersonate him while he fled the country. The overdose on the toilet was an accident that happened to an overzealous impersonator. He was never supposed to die; he was just supposed to impersonate Elvis until Elvis could devise a permanent plan to handle the Mafia.

OK. So some of my friends have delusional tendencies. It was to my amazement that Molly had laid low for twenty-five years and only recently began to fixate on Elvis.

Molly never did make that decision about her life and ended up staying at the day care center. She hated it. She didn't have a passion for children. She wanted to become a writer or an actress. It was obvious that she had the creativity for both—she was just stuck. Once her parents died, her brother moved to California, and Molly was left with the responsibility of running the center. Molly transferred the childcare tasks to another employee and focused on the administrative tasks.

Molly was also a single mother. She had a hostile relationship with her sixteen-year-old daughter at best. Molly sarcastically referred to her daughter as the Princess, while her daughter referred to Molly as the Queen Mum. Molly's ex-husband lived in a nearby town but offered little emotional or financial support. Molly was depressed and spent her life working, eating, and reading.

The Elvis obsession appeared to come out of nowhere, but seemed to be fueled by her recent interest with the Internet. She had purchased a computer of late and began surfing for Elvis sites. She soon began talking about Elvis sightings, even a few in Michigan's own beloved Kalamazoo. Our conversations became one-sided and consisted mainly of Molly's latest theory of where Elvis was lurking. According to Molly, Elvis occasionally impersonated himself in Vegas, just to keep the public guessing. Molly also spoke of her Web site family, other people, mainly women, who believed as she did about Elvis. They were attempting to gather signatures on a petition to give the American public access to an unheard-of single that Elvis had made. Molly wanted me to sign the petition. I was torn. I didn't really care whether the American public had access to this recording or not, yet if I signed, would I be enabling Molly's addiction? I signed under pressure from Molly.

Sometimes Molly did have an altruistic twist to her Elvis obsession. One time, she gathered donations for an orphanage in Nevada. According to Molly, Elvis frequented this orphanage whenever he performed in Las Vegas. Molly's work was "all in the name of Elvis," she told me. She couldn't wait to plan another act in the name of her idol, someone whom she now referred to as "my baby" or "my man" or "my lover." She spent most of her free time online chatting with her Web family, exchanging fantasies, anecdotes, film clips, and CDs. She had once told me that she had over 365 pictures of Elvis, which she had either framed individually or grouped together and decoupaged.

"One for each day of the year," she said. I could just imagine what her house looked like. She didn't invite me over much anymore, although she did invite me over one time for a five-hour marathon of Elvis movies. I respectfully declined. I had my own marathon to train for, a 26.2-mile run which I was completing in the name of the Stroke Association. I hadn't seen Molly in months.

This particular day, I had stopped by Molly's house to drop off some tomatoes. My tomato plant was flourishing, and I couldn't keep up with its production. I rang Molly's bell, but there was no answer. I waited a minute, then knocked. Still no answer. I knew someone was home—I could hear Elvis music blaring from the back room. I tried the doorknob. It was unlocked, so I let myself in.

"Hello," I called, "anyone home?" No answer. I followed my way through the house to the source of the Elvis concert in the study. There I found Molly sitting in front of her computer. She looked awful. She had gained some weight and had become a chain-smoker. A lit cigarette lay in the ashtray to her right, which was overflowing with cigarette butts. A jumbo pop was to her left. Empty carryout boxes were strewn about, as well as empty potato chip and pretzel bags. A half-empty bag of crackers lay at her feet. She was still in her pajamas, although it was in the early evening.

Molly looked up at me, unfazed, and stated, "Oh, hi! Just chatting with one of my online sisters. Didn't hear you . . . ," she trailed off. She hit Send and stared at the screen. It only took a second before she burst out laughing. She pointed to the screen and stated, "That Pelvisgirl is something else!"

Molly, a.k.a. Suspiciousminds, explained that they had been chatting about their sexual fantasies and what they would do to Elvis if they ever ran into him. Although Suspiciousminds offered me the opportunity to read their discourse, I only glanced at Pelvisgirl's last response, which was, "I never knew anyone else out there was as perverted as I was. Suspicious, you rock!" I was nauseous and wanted to heave my tomatoes. This, I decided not to do. I just looked at the screen, looked at Molly, and then looked back at the screen again.

Molly began talking, but I really didn't listen that closely. I heard bits and pieces: "I value your opinion, but I disagree with your assessment of my behavior . . . I called my former therapist after I spoke with you, and she thought my interest in Elvis was healthy . . ."

Between my own thoughts and Elvis singing in the background, I discerned that Molly was justifying her behavior, and that she would find other people to support her addictive behavior. "My online sisters agree . . . ," she continued.

I looked around the room. Every nook and cranny was filled with a picture of Elvis. Above the computer was a picture of young Elvis illuminated by a small light. Next to it was an illuminated picture of George W. Bush. Both lights were controlled by a special system so that Molly could clap her hands in any part of the room and the lights would turn on. It was apparent that Molly had spent a lot of time on these projects. She followed my gaze and explained that her sisters had sent her some of the pictures. "In this one, my baby is singing . . . and in this one, my love is . . . and this one, my man . . ." I couldn't hear anymore. I put the tomatoes down and placed my hands over my ears. I yelled, "Those drums! Those drums! Those incessant drums!" Molly just looked at me. I didn't know how else to get her attention but to quote a line from, what was it, *King Kong*?

"Molly, I'm worried about you," I said. "Look at you! You're a wreck. All you talk about is Elvis. You live, breathe, and play Elvis! Don't you ever take a break? What's with the chain-smoking, the pop, and the food? What's with the sex talk? What happened to your life?" I asked sternly. Molly began to cry.

"Please don't yell at me," she said.

I calmed down. "I'm just worried about you. We don't seem to have anything in common anymore. All you talk about is Elvis. You don't listen to me on the phone anymore, instead, I hear you clicking way on the computer! If Elvis were alive today, you'd be a stalker!"

Molly jumped up and ran to the bathroom. I could hear her retching and decided to wait it out.

"Are you all right?" I yelled.

"I'm fine. Go away," she replied. I left and didn't hear from Molly again.

I ran into Molly's daughter at the grocery store sometime later. She told me that Molly had developed an eating disorder. Molly had gained so much weight; she decided to buy a treadmill. She could always pop in an Elvis video while she worked out, but the treadmill didn't last long as it prohibited her from communicating with her online sisters. So the treadmill gathered dust while Molly began purging. She would sit in front of the computer for hours, smoke, eat, and vomit. Her daughter finally left and moved in with her father—she couldn't tolerate Molly's behavior any longer.

At first, Molly was keen to the notion of the Princess moving away—with her daughter gone, she would have no one complaining about her behavior. Unfortunately, with her daughter gone, Molly became so immersed with her Internet family that she began neglecting her bills. Molly ignored the bill collectors and eventually lost her house. She moved in with her brother. Back in Michigan, her brother had one stipulation—that she enter mental health therapy. Molly reluctantly agreed. No news on how the therapy is progressing, but I wonder if her therapist still believes that Molly's addiction is healthy.

Molly's daughter told me that she "got her good" before she left Molly's home. She stated that she turned all the pictures backward and unscrewed the lightbulbs. I couldn't get the image of Molly clapping her hands out of my mind.

Molly and her daughter still aren't talking.

That's where things stand now with Molly. As for me, I've developed an aversion to tomatoes. I've also completed my first marathon and am training for my second. I'm currently running ten miles per day and am gradually increasing my mileage—you don't think . . . you don't think that I'm spending too much time running, do you?

Does Anyone Speak Chinese?

I'm not a big fan of the state that begins with *F*. Every time I've visited, something unpleasant has happened. The first time I traveled there, I stuffed six hormone-laden college juniors in my 1972 Dodge Dart for a twenty-three-hour drive to the city that begins with *Fort*. It was spring break, and we were ready for adventure. With wall-to-wall college students, the streets were so packed one couldn't walk without being squished or trampled upon. To top it off, a majority of the students were drunk and belligerent—a peaceful environment it was not! I remember one such walk as my friends and I were attempting to locate a restaurant. I wasn't really paying attention. I was just trying to remain in an upright position (I had not been drinking) when I heard one of my friends gasp. This was followed by a slew of expletives from a boy who had been groping the girls as they walked by.

"#@! Why do I always get the fat ones?!" he barked. I turned around to see the blind swimmer—yes, it was the blind swimmer from my own university, being a jerk and cursing my good friend. The same blind swimmer who threw a pop machine out of a seven-story window for fun (so the story goes) and who put Limburger cheese through the ventilation system in my dormitory. This boy was not happy, and he appeared to take pride in making others unhappy as well. *Of all the people we could run into here*, I thought. I began to defend my friend, but she stopped me. She wanted to get out of there as fast as possible.

That was the first time I visited the state that begins with *F*. The second time, my boyfriend came down with a wicked ear infection, and I came down with the flu. We spent the entire week holed up in the hotel room. (I tell you, we suffered on that flight back home!)

The third time, it rained for two days straight on a visit to Disney World. Unfortunately, our visit only lasted two days. On the first day, we noticed a family walking through the park wearing garbage bags (even on their feet!). We thought, *what a great, economical idea!* On day two, we arrived clad in black plastic bags. First of all, do you know how ridiculous one looks, clad in garbage bags? Second, do you know how slippery walking in the rain with plastic on your feet can be? And third, do you know that rain will soak you to the bone regardless if you're wearing plastic?

All these examples were really not the fault of the state that begins with *F*. So when the opportunity afforded itself for me to travel to the city that begins with *M* in the state that begins with *F*, I was only slightly apprehensive. What possible unpleasantness could I experience this time? It was January, and the warm sunshine beckoned to me.

Still active with the Stroke Association and their marathoning program, I planned on joining my team, which had left the previous day, in the *M* city. I used some frequent-flyer miles and traveled by myself. Since I was not with the team, I would have to secure my own transportation from the airport to the hotel. I had called the hotel and discovered that they did not have their own shuttle. They recommended taking either an airport shuttle or a taxi. I opted for the airport shuttle as it was cheaper.

I saw a shuttle sitting at the curb and quickly ran up to it. I opened the door and asked the driver if he had space for another passenger. There were only two occupants besides the driver. Both occupants wore blue suits and appeared to be pilots. The driver turned to me but did not say a word. He rubbed his fingers together and smirked. I stared at him briefly, thinking that he wanted to get paid.

One of the pilots said to me, "You have to go to the desk first and get a ticket." He pointed to a small desk approximately twenty-five feet away. I wondered why the driver had not told me so himself.

I walked to the desk where a short slightly overweight woman was sitting. She was staring into space and looked bored. I told her that I wanted to take the shuttle to the Hyatt. She looked at me, smacked her lips, and proceeded to write. When I handed her my money, she shook her head and pointed to the shuttle. My patience was running thin.

"Is everyone here so rude?" I asked.

"Huh?" the woman replied. I didn't clarify.

"Where do I go now?" I sighed.

"Just wait," she said.

I walked over to the curb. In the meantime, the shuttle driver approached the woman, said something in Spanish, and threw up his arms. The woman, slightly frazzled, ignored him and began examining the tickets of other patrons who were also waiting for instructions.

"Hey, big momma!" she cried to me.

"Me?" I asked, pointing to myself. "You're calling me big momma?" Huh! Little did she realize that I only weighed 125 pounds even if I did have endowed buttocks! The woman walked over to me, grabbed my ticket, glanced at it, and quickly returned it. The driver said something again in Spanish, which I assumed was cursing, jumped in his van, and sped off. The woman returned to her seat, smacking her lips and rolling her head. Almost instantaneously, another van pulled up. This van, however, was packed with people. My eyes were fixed on the two children who were in the backseat. A wire mesh separated the backseat from the trunk space. The two children had their faces plastered to the wire mesh, apparently clinging on for dear life! I imagined that the wire mesh would permanently be tattooed on their cheeks. "Oh Lord, please don't let this be my shuttle!" I said to myself.

After some confusion, the driver began taking luggage. He spoke under his breath with every suitcase he grabbed. Since he had taken my luggage, I assumed that I should board. I opened the door and looked for a spot. There was one spot left.

"We have three people boarding," I said. No one moved. I repeated myself. This time, the man in the front seat unbuckled his seat belt and moved over one space. I took the spot next to him. A young woman took the seat next to me. The last woman took the spot next to the driver—she had to move his belongings to sit down. As we were getting situated, the driver asked for the tickets of the people in the back. He repeated himself as an elderly man handed the driver his ticket.

The driver began speaking loudly and slowly to the man.

"I . . . need . . . to know . . . the address . . . of where . . . you're going," the driver said. The man pointed to the ticket.

"No. The address, the address!" the driver yelled. I glanced over my shoulder. The man was a foreigner, appeared to be Asian, and obviously didn't understand the driver. *Have pity on the man*, I thought to myself. I turned around and asked, "Does anyone speak Chinese?" Silence. *Does anyone speak, period?* I thought to myself. But my thoughts were interrupted by the driver once more.

"Chinese? This man is Hispanic!" the driver said to me. I looked at the man again and discovered that the driver was correct. I cringed and prayed that I would just melt into the seat until we arrived at the Hyatt. *What is with this state that begins with an* F? I thought.

The driver jumped into the van and began speaking Spanish to the man. He drove approximately ten feet before he pulled over. "All this paperwork . . . ," he said. He proceeded to complete his paperwork, and twenty minutes later, we were on the road. I reached the Hyatt 1½ hours later after dodging traffic and avoiding a side-on collision with a car. I was exhausted and looking forward to relaxing with my team.

The marathon went well; I had a lot of fun, and the time had come to say goodbye to my teammates. My teammates left before I did, so I had some time to explore the surroundings on my own. I had seen these surroundings plenty of times over the weekend, and I wanted to stop by a grocery store I had noticed earlier. I found the grocery store; but somehow, for some reason, I became disorientated. I knew that the hotel was only a few blocks away, but nothing looked familiar. I saw a hot dog vendor opening up his stand. A young woman was with him, helping him open.

"Excuse me," I said. "I know that the Hyatt is around here somewhere, but I'm a little confused."
The woman looked at me and asked, "The Hyatt what?"
"The Hyatt Regency," I said. She looked at me blankly and turned to the man.
"Can I help you?" he asked.
"Yes. I'm lost. I'm looking for the Hyatt. I know it's around here somewhere."
The man looked puzzled.
"The Hyatt what?" he asked me.
"The Hyatt Regency Hotel," I answered.
"What are you asking me for?" the man responded curtly. "Is it that one?" He pointed briskly to a building across the street. "No," I said. "Thank you for your time." I turned away, frustrated. Down the street, I asked a man in a blue suit (who did not appear to be a pilot, by the way). He pointed in the

opposite direction and told me that I was only two blocks away. I thanked him and vowed never to purchase a hot dog from that vendor—ever—if I could find the location again.

I made it back to the hotel, finished packing my bags, and grabbed a taxi to the airport. I made small talk with the driver, who I discovered was from Barbados. Although he had been in the country for eighteen years, he only spoke broken English. "How you like warm weather?" he asked me.

"I miss the snow," I replied.

"Yes, is good to be away from snow," he answered. I stifled a scream and looked out of the window.

The rest of my trip was uneventful, except that I had a layover in Houston. This made no sense to me since my destination was Detroit. By that time, all I wanted to do was reach my home and jump into my warm bed.

Six hours later, I was able to do just that.

Oh, by the way, did you know that some marathoners wear plastic bags while they're waiting for the race to begin? The bags provide warmth from the chilly morning air and are quite easy to remove once the race begins. At my last race in Detroit, I noticed a woman wearing a full-length garbage bag—I've got to get my hands on one!

Becoming Mother

It's every woman's nightmare: one day you wake up and realize that you've become your mother. You go through life, especially in your teen years, thinking that you will never become your mother. At that time, you believe that your mother is old-fashioned, doesn't understand you, and is stuck in her ways. You vow that you will never turn into your mother, and you even tell her so! Then, one day something happens, and you suddenly realize that it's happened—you've turned into your mother.

My first such realization came when I was in my midthirties. I was working as a therapist in a mental health agency. My boss was a very bright psychologist who enjoyed playing chess and table tennis. He was very skilled at working with our consumers, and I always looked forward to consulting with him.

One morning, he decided to finally assemble the bookcase that he had ordered for his office. I paid no attention to this as I had a busy schedule.

At noon, a coworker informed me, "You know, Harry still doesn't have that bookcase assembled. I told him that he should ask you to put it together. You'd have it done in no time! He said he didn't need your help," she added. "Whenever I walked down the hallway, I saw him hunched over the instructions, so I would yell out your name. He finally shut his door when he saw me coming!"

I was shocked. Not that he had refused to seek my help, but that she would suggest that I was skilled at such things. Where did she get that idea from? Of course, I had just recently put together my own bookcase at home, and I did crawl up on my roof to repair some loose shingles; but didn't everyone do these things? Yes, of course! I'm single. Who else will do these things for me? Why would I hire a private contractor to complete projects that I can complete myself?

No, the larger shock was that I was displaying behavior that described my mother. My mother is a strong, independent woman. Living on a horse farm, she has learned to depend on herself for much of the physical labor. My mom converted a two-car garage into a small barn, repaired fences, chopped wood, and built a training "horse" out of a barrel for her mounted gymnastics team. My mother is very creative and skilled with deciphering problems. I am creative, independent, and skilled with deciphering certain problems but have no patience for deciphering instructions.

When had I turned into my mother?

The other day, I noticed that I had developed a small blister on my right foot after I had completed five miles at the gym.

Looks like it's time to buy new running shoes, I thought. I jumped in the shower and attempted to dry my hair. The hair dryer was broken however, so I had to leave with wet hair. It was warm outside, so I drove with my windows down, allowing the air to dry my hair. I had other errands to complete before I hit the running store, and was famished and tired by the time I reached my destination. I decided to eat first. Now let me tell you that I normally do not eat at fast-food restaurants. I don't eat hamburgers and fries frequently, although every now and then they hit the spot. It just so happens that a fast-food restaurant is directly across the parking lot from the running store. As I parked my car, I debated whether to go for the fast food.

"I'm starving," I said.

"Yes, but fast food is so unhealthy," I replied.

"But you're training for a marathon," I countered.

"Ah, but only a half marathon!" I reasoned.

"But you'll burn the calories off," I said.

"When? You just finished working out. You should have thought of this before you trained."

I entered the restaurant.

When I reached the counter, a nice young girl of about twenty waited on me.

"I'll take the number 1 small, no cheese, with a Diet Coke," I said.

"That will be $4," she informed me.

I looked up at the menu.

"Are you sure that's right? The menu says that the number 1 costs—"

She cut me off, "I gave you the senior discount."

"Senior discount?" I asked.

"Yes, everyone fifty and over gets the senior discount," she replied.

"Fifty!" I barked. "You think I'm fifty?"

The girl stood staring at me.

"Oh my god!" I said. "You don't think I'm fifty—you think I'm over fifty!"

The girl left the register to retrieve my meal. I stood there in disbelief that this twentysomething girl thought I was a senior citizen. She didn't know that I was old enough to be her mother yet one whole year younger than fifty. She didn't know that I was probably in better shape physically than she was—I was a marathoner after all!

She returned with my food. I retrieved my license.

"Look," I said to her, "here's my license. I'm not fifty."

"That will be $4," she said. "Have a nice day."

I gave her $4 and sat down, disgusted, shaking my head in disbelief. *It must be my hair*, I thought—after all, it was windblown. I shoved the burger in my mouth, followed by the fries. *Who does that girl think she is?* I thought further. *Fifty! Huh!*

I suddenly remembered an incident that occurred shortly before my mother's fiftieth birthday. She had also gone into a fast-food restaurant and was given the senior discount. She was so upset by that incident; she talked about it for days.

I finished my meal, threw away my refuse, and walked out the door.

"Why did you just gorge on a hamburger and fries?" I asked myself. "You're going to regret it."

"But you're training for a marathon." I answered.

"That's a half marathon." I replied.

The Man with the Tattoos

The man with the tattoos stopped to talk to me today. I didn't even see him at first. I was in "the zone," power walking to the track, when I heard a voice call out to me. I was startled from my trance and immediately recognized him. When my dog was young, we would pass this man and his wife while taking our morning walks. He appeared to be in his sixties even then, a friendly man with graying hair, glasses, and multiple tattoos that accented his muscular arms. His hair was in a buzz cut, and I imagined that he had been in the military. His wife was very quiet and appeared to be older than he. She was short, wore glasses, and walked with a limp. We always passed her by, although my dog could barely walk in his last days.

"Where's your dog?" the man yelled to me. He was in his red pickup truck, and the window was rolled down. I frequently saw the man with the tattoos in his driveway, washing and waxing the truck. It was always clean and shiny.

I raised my hand to my ear.

"Where's your dog?" he repeated.

"Oh," I said, "he died. I had to put him down."
"What was he, ten years old?" the man asked.

I approached the truck, willing to break my workout in order to reminisce about my beloved dog. "No, fourteen. He was old and in a lot of pain. It was time."

"Fourteen. Oh. He could hardly move," he added.

"Yes," I said. "His last days were difficult."

I explained to the man how the vet initially thought he was treatable and that she had prescribed pain medication for his arthritis. I explained to the man that the medication only worked one week, and then he was back to being in excruciating pain. I wanted to explain how grateful I was that the vet came out to my house to put him down and that he died from liver failure, not arthritis. I wanted to tell the man that my vet had nicknamed him "miracle dog" because he survived a wicked case of encephalitis when he was nine. I wanted to let the man know that it truly had been a miracle that my dog found me thirteen years previously, and had he not slept by my car in the parking lot at work, I never would have rescued him. He might not have survived the snowstorm that came through that night, but the man interrupted me. I don't know if he couldn't bear hearing about it or if he just wanted to change the subject, but then he began telling me about his own German shepherd. He told me that the dog only lasted eight months in his household before he gave him away. The man believed the dog to be crazy because all he liked to do was run in circles. One day, the man was so stressed by the dog's behavior that he threw a hammer at him.

"Thank God I missed," he said. "I knew I had to get rid of him before I killed him. Well, nice talking to yah!" And that was it. The conversation was over before it had even started. The man drove away, and I remained distracted for the rest of my workout.

A friend of mine reading this story informed me that the ending left her hanging. That was the point. The man with the tattoos had interrupted my workout and redirected my focus to the grief over my dog. He had supplied little support or empathy, just opened the wounds at a time when I had still been vulnerable to obsessing about my loss. Unlike him, I didn't have a hammer to throw.

Instead, I had to throw myself into my workout.

The Pillow

Today was a bad day. I woke up with a migraine—although I immediately took some medication, I continued to suffer for the remainder of the day. Most of my time was spent sleeping in the comfort of my sunroom, with Angelo at my head.

Who is Angelo?

Angelo is the stray cat that I rescued two winters ago. I had noticed Angelo coming around for quite some time before I took the courage to welcome him into my life. I say *courage* because I already had three cats (yes, all strays). I didn't know how they would relate to each other, I didn't know if Angelo had any communicable diseases, and I didn't know if I wanted the responsibility of taking care of another cat! He stole my heart that day, however, when he snuck into my house. It was frigid cold, and like a Scud missile seeking its target, he honed in on the warmth of my home. He saw his opportunity when I was struggling to close the patio door. Angelo quickly darted through my legs. Once inside, he cautiously scoped out his surroundings. Much to my surprise, my other cats approached him, sniffed him, and turned away. Angelo then happily rubbed up against my legs. When I leaned over to pet him, I discovered that he was declawed. I took pity on him, and the rest is history.

I love my sunroom. It's big, warm, has lots of windows, and is filled with plants. I lay down on the sofa after briefly running to the bank, a fifteen-minute errand that wore me out. I debated on whether to turn the ceiling fan off but decided to keep it on. I covered myself with not one, but two blankets to ward off the chill that was slowly taking over my body—this, despite the fact that it was eighty-three degrees outside and my air-conditioning was turned off. I curled up in the fetal position under the blankets when Angelo made his move. He had been watching me from across the room and waited until I became sufficiently comfortable before he approached me. I could hear him approaching before he actually reached the sofa, his loud and rhythmic purring letting me know of his intentions. Within seconds, he would jump onto the sofa by my head and begin kneading my scalp. This was one of his favorite things to do, albeit one of my least favorite, especially with a migraine. He jumped up and circled my head. He finally chose a spot that was conducive to head kneading and began pawing at my scalp. I could feel the pounding of the migraine behind my left eye. Angelo ran his paws through my hair and continued to purr. Soon, the pounding of the migraine and the rhythm of Angelo's strokes became one. I imagined myself on a boat and could hear the coxswain yelling, "Stroke! Stroke! Stroke!"

I was hoping that we would reach our destination quickly and that the stroking would end soon. Oddly enough, I began to feel a slight relief with every pull from Angelo. I didn't have the energy to stop him anyway, so I allowed him to continue. Like a massage therapist, Angelo changed positions, moved to my shoulder, and began kneading my temple. He stroked my temple two or three times, stopped, lay down, and kept his paw on my face. *What, done so soon?* I thought in earnest. Angelo leaned over, purred in my ear, and laid his head down. "Yes," he answered. "And now you've become my pillow!"

Secret Santa

I'm in my own therapy session sitting on a love seat. I'm very tired and just about to fall asleep when the bearded fat lady from the circus sits down next to me. She is so large; she takes up the rest of the space on the love seat. She is lethargic in her movement and sits on the edge of the love seat for fear she will not be able to stand back up on her own. I, in the meantime, in my own lethargy, have sunken down on the love seat so that only my body from the waist up is resting on the furniture. It is the intention of the bearded fat lady to use me as a lever to lift herself up when needed. I feel myself slowly rolling closer to the armrest due to the weight of the bearded fat lady. I know if I reach the armrest, I will suffocate. Somehow, I am able to see that my Secret Santa is standing across the room. She is smiling at me and is the most friendly, caring, kind, and compassionate person I know.

No time to wonder why my Secret Santa or therapist is not helping me. I wake with a start to find that Angelo has wrapped his body around my head again and is kneading me with his paws. I'm at the edge of my bed and am about to fall onto the floor. "OK, bearded fat lady," I tell him, "scoot over." I push the cat over and attempt to fall back asleep.

But I can't. Instead, I try to analyze the dream and wonder why my Secret Santa is in it.

I love participating in Secret Santa. When I was a child, my mother participated in Secret Pal with the Women's Auxiliary at church. She always seemed to get pleasure in leaving cryptic notes and reveled in the challenge it took for her friends to decipher them. I looked forward to doing the same when I became an adult. The thing is, at my place of employment, I am the only one who takes the time to leave clues about my identity prior to the Christmas party. For me, having someone else go crazy over cracking my identity is what it's all about.

This year, the recipient of my clues was not able to attend the Christmas party. As a result, I exposed my identity to her prior to the party. I went to her office with my "big" gift with the intention of keeping the ruse on—I was not her Secret Santa, but was sent by her Secret Santa to deliver the gift. Unfortunately, my recipient was very clever and had figured it out before I even opened my mouth.

"You know," she said, "you were the best Secret Santa ever!"

"Oh really?" I asked.

"Yes," she said. "Last year was a real bummer. My Secret Santa didn't get me anything. Nothing at all. Not a card, a note, or an e-mail. Nothing. I sat there like a fool at the party while everyone else was having fun and opening their gifts."

"Wow, that's weird!" I said. "Did you find out who your Secret Santa was?"

"Yes," she said. "That was probably the weirdest thing of all. She approached me, told me she was my Secret Santa, smiled, and walked away. I was left dumbfounded."

I felt sorry for my recipient. "Maybe she didn't get it . . . Well I'm glad you enjoyed my small gifts and my notes. How did you figure out it was me?"

"It was your clue about your dreams," she said. "You are the only person I know who has vivid, humorous, and bizarre dreams and remembers them!"

My recipient opened her "big" gift and thanked me for my consideration. I walked back to my office wondering why someone would sign up for Secret Santa and then not buy a gift. When I returned to my office, I told my office mate what had happened.

"I know," she said. "We felt so badly for her that a few of us pitched in and bought her something."

"What about her Secret Santa? Did she ever give an explanation?" I asked.

"No," she said.

That night at the Christmas party, my office mate nudged me and pointed to a girl who was sitting across the table from us. She was wildly text messaging someone and was not interacting with anyone else.

"She's the one," my office mate told me. I just shook my head.

A few weeks later, I was talking to the text messaging girl in her office. We had a pleasant conversation about politics. While she was speaking, I perused her office for a clue as to why she would not follow the rules of Secret Santa. If there was a clue, I didn't find it. Her office consisted of the normal office paraphernalia: computer, printer, phone, etc. I left disappointed. Later,

I wondered if she realized what I had been up to. I thought, *Maybe she got a kick out of me trying to figure her logic out. Maybe, for her, the joy is not in having others figure out her identity but in figuring out her motivation.*

Well that might explain why my recipient never received a gift from the text messaging girl, but that doesn't explain why my Secret Santa was in my dream.

I'm just glad that I woke up before I fell onto the floor.

Yours Very Truly

I come from a long line of practical jokers. As far back as I can remember, my family always played jokes on one another. One joke is caught on tape and occurred while we were camping at Point Pelee. My sister found an Inspected by Number 12 sticker on her new sweatshirt as she unpacked it. She thought it would be funny to silently stick it on the back of my other sister while we were walking along the beach. I witnessed her skillfulness as she successfully placed the sticker on my sister's back. I later witnessed my other sister discovering the sticker and placing it on my brother's back. What I didn't witness was my brother skillfully placing the sticker on my back. I didn't notice it until it was time to sleep, but my mother had captured it all on film: here I am, dodging the waves when my brother pretends to run into me, and I'm suddenly tagged with the sticker. Oh, and look, here we are hours later on another part of the beach. I run in front of the camera, make a face, then turn around and run the other way. What's on my back? Inspector 12!

My father was not one for physical jokes but was always cracking jokes or making plays on words. For example, whenever we came to a Do Not Pass sign, he would inform us that we were entering the Doughnut Pass. This taught us to always be on the lookout for hidden meanings in words. Whenever we came upon a sign that had our name on it, part of our name on it, or even our initials on it, all the inhabitants of the car had to salute that person. For example, if I saw an A&W Root Beer Stand, I would announce, "Salute to A&W!" as these were the initials of my middle names. Everyone then would salute me as we drove by the stand.

My mother was more for the physical jokes. She once helped my eldest sister convince the neighborhood children that there was an elf living in our house. My sister was in the backyard telling the children about an elf that lived in our tree. My mom, who was upstairs, overheard the conversation and just so happened to be sewing an elf that she was making as a Christmas gift for me. Although she had not completed sewing the elf, most of it was done, and one could clearly see that the figure was indeed an elf. Surprisingly, there had been no collaboration between my mother and my sister. My mom took it upon herself to take advantage of the situation, kneeled down under the open window, strategically placed the elf in the window, and began speaking to the children. The children began screaming, "Elfie! Elfie!" and ran home with excitement, happily telling their parents about the elf at our house.

The next day when they returned, they called for the elf again. My mother obliged them for two days, but then the visitation of Elfie stopped. Apparently, a few of the children were having nightmares, so my mother decided to stop traumatizing them.

The most notorious of practical jokes, however, was delivered by my brother. My brother was attending school at a small college on the outskirts of Ann Arbor. He wanted to become a minister. The campus sat along the banks of the Huron River. One day as he was walking along the bank, he was inspired to pull a prank on one of his roommates. I don't know where he got this idea from, but he decided to take a small boulder that was lying along the river, roll it up the embankment, through a small field, carry it into his dorm room, and place it into his own bed. Of course, what he was doing was framing his roommate. When the roommate came home, he accused him of placing the boulder in his bed. The roommate denied it; but by this time, my brother's other roommates were in on the joke, and they all turned on the poor guy. Eventually the truth came out, which started a long string of paybacks.

My most notorious prank came when I was in my early twenties. I had just graduated from the university and had not yet landed a job in my field. Instead, I was working as a secretary at a bank in the loan department. Now banking is fine and dandy, but it's not my passion. I was incredibly bored with typing overdue letters. I needed some action, some excitement in my life. One day I found it.

The year was 1980. As I sat at my typewriter, I became more frustrated with the errors that I was typing. It was almost lunchtime; I was hungry and was careless with my work. Although I made the corrections as I went along, I was not satisfied with the final product. I thought that the loan officer would also be dissatisfied with the completed letter, so I deliberately decided to change the closing. Instead of typing "Yours Very Truly," I typed "Love and Kisses." I placed the letter and envelope on the loan officer's desk for signature and went to lunch—Oh, I forgot to tell you that the loan officer was female, and the client was male.

I expected to find the unsigned letter sitting on my desk when I returned, but it was not there. Likewise, I expected some comment from the loan officer, but none arrived. Finally, I asked her myself.

"So," I stated, "how did you like the letter to Mr. Smith?"

The loan officer peered over her glasses.

"It was fine," she stated. I smiled at her broadly as I thought she was joking with me.

"You liked it?" I inquired.

"Yes," she said. Suddenly, I realized she was being truthful. A mild panic began to overtake me.

"What did you do with the letter?" I queried.

"I signed it and sent it to the mail room," she replied.

I was told that I lost all color in my cheeks at that moment, but who is to say? All I know is that I raced down to that mail room as fast as I could. I had never been down to the mail room before, so I wasn't quite certain where I was headed. I stopped twice to catch my breath and ask for directions. I finally reached my destination after what seemed like hours. As I burst through the door, hysteria set in. I was faced with stacks upon stacks of mail. What was I to do? Where was I to begin?

The mail boy was making his rounds, so I could not ask for direction. I knew that I had to examine the letters systematically, so I decided to start with the stacks to my right and work left. I tried to calm myself down, for I knew that I might make an error if I did not. Five minutes of searching produced no letter.

I began to berate myself, "You stupid, stupid, idiot! You'd better find that letter. This could mean your job!" I said aloud. "Stop! Calm down! Just look for the letter," I told myself. Ten minutes went by. Fifteen minutes went by. Twenty minutes, and in walks the mail boy. He was just about as startled as I was to find someone in his mail room.

"I'm looking for a letter addressed to Mr. Smith that you picked up from the loan department between noon and ten!" I snapped. "Has that mail been processed yet?"

"No," he said. "It should be over here." The mail boy pointed to a stack on the left.

"Thank goodness!" I screamed. I rushed over to the stack and found the letter sitting on the very top. I ripped open the envelope to make certain that I indeed had the correct letter. "Dear Mr. Smith," I read. "You're past due, blah, blah, blah . . ." Suddenly I was conscious that I was reading aloud, so I changed what was actually written. "Yours Very Truly—yep! I have the right letter! Thank you for your help!" I turned away and wiped the sweat from my brow. That was a close call.

I slowly walked back to the loan department clutching my letter and avoiding all eye contact. Luckily, the loan officer was not at her desk when I returned. I tore the letter in half and quickly stuck it in my purse—I didn't want any incriminating evidence. I would take the letter home and really destroy it! I retyped the letter and envelope and hand delivered it to the loan officer.

"I'm sorry," I said to her. I knew that the loan officer sensed that something was wrong as I had fled without saying a word to her.

"That's OK," she replied. She just looked at me and smiled. I felt as if I should say more, but I really didn't want to for fear she would ask me to explain. "I . . . I . . . ," I stammered.

"Again, I'm sorry," I said.

"Don't worry about it," she responded.

I returned to my desk with a lump in my throat and a pit in my stomach. I worked very hard for the rest of the day and made certain that I didn't rush through any of my work. The loan officer didn't say anything more about the incident, and neither did I. In fact, the loan officer never said anything to me about it ever again. To this day, I don't know if she knew exactly what I had typed. It doesn't matter anymore. I learned my lesson. My brother can have the glory of being the most notorious prankster in my family!

Spucken!

One of the most amazing experiences I've had so far in my life was to witness kidney transplant surgery. Yes, believe it or not, I was right there in the operating room, standing on a wooden platform, looking over the shoulder of the transplant surgeon. I was standing so close to him; I wondered if he could feel my breath on his neck. This thought made me nervous as I didn't want to break his concentration. I found myself holding my breath on several occasions as a result. This didn't help much as the surgery lasted six hours. Luckily, I could take a break as I needed it—the poor surgeon could not. When the kidney was finally removed (I was in the donor's surgery), I was surprised to see that the kidney resembled a small fat-covered chicken. I had never actually envisioned what a kidney would look like before, but I guess I expected it to look like a very large lima bean. It did not. Not that it mattered. What mattered was that I was witness to this incredible event, that I found it fascinating, and that I didn't faint!

I had a very weak stomach as a child. I couldn't tolerate the sight of blood. I also couldn't tolerate anything to do with the nose or with anything slimy. Go figure. I remember visiting one of my patients in her hospital room around the same time that I witnessed the transplant surgery. She had a very large needle stuck in her nose, and a tube—well, I'm not divulging the rest. Suffice it to say, I quickly became queasy and almost passed out.

This had not been the first nasal-almost-passing-out experience I had had. The first happened seven years earlier.

I was living in Germany and was experiencing an overabundance of sinus problems. I was constantly getting sinus headaches and sinus infections. One day, I had had enough and decided to have my sinuses flushed as my doctor had recommended. Although I had been living in Germany for a year already, my command of medical terminology was basically nothing.

I remember sitting in my doctor's office, nodding my head as he explained what the procedure would entail. I threw in a "hmm" and an "ah" every now and then to make it look like I understood what he was saying. He threw in some English every now and then; but he, like me, didn't know the technical terminology. So what I understood was this: tube, inserted into nose, water, faucet, refreshing.

Sounded easy enough!

The day arrived for my procedure. I entered the office only slightly apprehensive. The nurse took me back into a room and was quite chatty with me once she determined I was from the States.

"No worries," she said to me in English. "All is well." She had her back to me as she said this, and when she turned around, I saw that she held a giant needle in her hand. When I say giant, I mean giant. The needle was at least six inches long. I am not exaggerating. It also had a red ball at the end of it, which made it look like a thermometer. As the nurse approached me, I felt myself backing into the wall.

"What are you doing with that?" I asked in German.

"No worries," she replied in English.

"This . . ." and then she made a shoving motion with her arm, and I immediately understood that she intended on shoving the needle up my nose. "No worries," she said again in English, and then she broke into German and explained that the needle was filled with something to numb my nose.

"Hmm," and, "ah," I said. What had I gotten myself into? Was this really worth it? By the time I had answered those questions, the nurse had plunged the needle into my nose. My immediate reflex was to pull back.

"Nein, nein!" she yelled. The nurse pulled me away from the wall where I had just left my imprint.

"Ow!" I yelled.

She grabbed my shoulder and continued to impale me with the needle. I felt a sharp sting radiate from my nostril to the bridge of my nose. The nurse struggled for a bit, moving the needle back and forth inside my nostril. What else could I do but acquiesce? You don't fight Nurse Ratchet when she has a needle up your nose.

I shut my eyes and began praying. *Please God; please let this go quickly and painlessly!* After one last twist of the needle, Nurse Ratchet left the room.

I sat there with my eyes closed for who knows how long. I was drenched in sweat. Suddenly, there came a knock on the door. I opened one eye, and then the other. The doctor entered, smiling broadly.

"You are a fighter," he said in English. "No worries. It is very simple," he continued. He attempted to explain again in English but became frustrated and broke into German. I interrupted him in German. I didn't want to know. I just wanted to get the procedure over with. I planned on keeping my eyes shut the entire time anyway, so onward and upward! He nodded his head, and I shut my eyes. I felt his hand on my shoulder as he gently pulled me to a standing position. *He wants me to move,* I thought. I didn't open my eyes but held my arms out in front of me in order to avoid bumping into anything. Of course, it would have been easier had I opened my eyes at that point, but I really didn't want to see what was awaiting me. He chuckled and led me across the room to another chair. I plopped down and heard the doctor turning some switches. He stood in front of me, and I thought that I felt something moving up my nostril again, but I couldn't be certain. Had he removed the needle? Had he replaced it with a tube? I couldn't tell. At least I wasn't in pain.

Suddenly, I heard it. I heard the water. I heard water running and a sucking noise like a vacuum cleaner. The next thing I felt was a burning sensation behind my eyes; and I could see, yes, actually see a river of water tumbling through my head. I kid you not! I saw a tumbling red river passing very quickly before my eyes. The burning flowed throughout my head, and then I felt it. I felt slime. I felt slime in my throat, and not just a little slime but the Grand Canyon full of slime. *Oh god!* I thought, *I'm going to vomit!*

"Spucken!" the doctor said. "Spucken, Spucken, Spucken!" he now yelled at me.

"What the hell?" I asked myself. "I'm trying not to vomit, and he's yelling some new word at me!"

Suddenly, it hit me that he wanted me to spit. I opened my eyes and saw a sink next to me—the kind that you used to see at dentists' offices. I quickly leaned over and spat.

"Raus Spucken!" he continued to yell at me. He rolled his *r* and repeated, "Raus Spucken!" My doctor had turned into Colonel Klink. Needless to say, I spat in that sink for a very long time, all the while feeling nauseous and panicky.

Forty-five minutes later, it was all over with, and I was spent. I leaned back in my chair and placed my head in my hand. Still queasy, I closed my eyes. I felt my doctor's hand on my shoulder as Nurse Ratchet entered the room again. He told her to accompany me to the waiting room as I was still very fragile. (Now this I understood!) The nurse lifted me out of my chair and guided me into the waiting area. I glanced into a mirror before I sat down. My face was pale, and I had a thermometer sticking out of my nose. That was it! I could feel all the life being drained out of me and my knees beginning to buckle. Nurse Ratchet would have nothing of it however. She began yelling at me and pulling at my arms. Somehow, I snapped out of it and sat down, slumped over my lap. *I'll never do this again!* I thought.

And I never did.

And I never forgot the word *Spucken.*

My Beautiful Red Car

I was visiting my best friends one night when one of their friends decided to stop over. He was the owner of an Egyptian restaurant and had brought over some food. My eyes caught sight of several round balls, slightly smaller than my fist. I don't remember what color the balls were, but if I recall correctly, their texture was wrinkled. I asked the restaurant owner what they were, but since his German was worse than mine, he didn't understand my question. My Egyptian friend translated and told me they were camels' eyes. I knew immediately that they were not camels' eyes and couldn't tell if it was my friend who was trying to fool me or the owner of the restaurant. I turned to my other friend, who was German, and she just rolled her eyes. I picked up a ball, rolled it in my palm, and smelled it. Both my Egyptian friend and the restaurant owner encouraged me to eat it. I started to take a small bite, but they both protested and instructed me to place the entire ball in my mouth. My German friend warned me not to trust these two scoundrels, but I decided to take the risk. I placed the entire ball in my mouth and bit into it.

It was a hot pepper.

Juice squirted everywhere. My mouth and throat immediately caught on fire. Tears welled from my eyes. I grabbed my throat and started coughing. I leaned over and spat the pepper onto my plate. My German friend handed me some bread and told me to stay away from the water. I stuffed the bread in my mouth and begged for more. The two scoundrels laughed. I paced and tried to work off the pain. I'd never trust those two again!

It was the early 1980s, and I was living in West Berlin. It was an exciting time for me. I was living in a foreign country, learning German, and becoming an independent woman. I had only had one year of German in college before I moved to Germany, didn't personally know anyone living in Berlin, and had never even been on a plane before. What an experience!

I remember walking down the street one day in a section of town that I usually didn't frequent. I had attempted to locate a used bookstore but was unable to find it. On my way back to the subway station, I noticed a man in a red car driving very slowly down the street. He caught my eye because he was very animated while driving. As he rolled to a stop, he waved his hands in the air wildly and cocked his head to and fro. I assumed that he was listening to the radio and was really enjoying whatever song was playing. I laughed as I crossed in front of him. The man turned right and proceeded very slowly down the street, tailing me. He followed me briefly, then honked his horn and motioned to me. I stopped and looked at him. Did I know him? He had curly black hair, wore sunglasses, and smiled profusely. Wait, was it Mac?

Mac was a man that frequented a restaurant that I worked at. He was from Hawaii.

Yes, it was Mac. I waved to him and approached the car. As I neared the car, however, I realized that it was indeed not Mac. I shook my head and retreated. The subway entrance was just a few feet away. I walked down the stairs, validated my ticket, and entered the last car of an awaiting train. As I waited for the train to depart, I could hear someone running down the stairs. The person jumped into the car just as the doors shut. It was him. It was the man in the red car.

My heart began to pound. What was he doing here?

The man looked at me and grinned. He rocked his head back and forth and waved at me. Although I ignored him, it did no good. The man approached me but did not say a word—he just stood in front of me and stared. I began to sweat. What was I to do? What did he want? Why was he following me? I felt trapped.

I moved to the other end of the car. The man did not follow me but continued to stare at me. My thoughts raced. I was in an unfamiliar part of town. I had no idea where the closest police station was. It was the middle of the day during the middle of the week. My best friends were working, and their places of employment were nowhere near a subway station. I decided to go to a shoe store where another friend of mine worked. The store was near Bahnhof Zoo. Hopefully, my friend would be working, and she could call the police.

The only problem was that I had to make a transfer.

I counted the stops before my transfer and devised a plan. When it came time for me to disembark, I hesitated so that the man would not know that I planned on leaving the car. I counted to ten, then bolted from the car. I ran up the stairs, pushing through the crowds, saying, "Excuse me . . . pardon me . . . excuse me," all the way. I didn't dare look behind me, but when the crowds began to thin, I heard someone running up from behind me. I ran down the next set of stairs to the train platform, hoping there would be a crowd of people. Unfortunately, there was none.

I looked to the left and looked to the right. There was not a soul in sight. I panicked.

The man approached me and whispered in my ear, "Why do you run from me? Come with me in my beautiful red car!"

My heart was pounding, and I was drenched in sweat.

I ignored the man.

He then spoke in broken English, "My car . . . is red . . . I love you."

Just then, I heard footsteps approaching. A tall man with blonde hair turned the corner and headed toward a nearby bench. He wore glasses and had a newspaper under his arm. I didn't have time to think. I threw up my arms and yelled to this man in German, "Cousin Klaus! There you are. So happy to see you. I thought maybe I had the wrong station."

The man looked at me, puzzled. "I think you have the wrong person," he said and began opening his newspaper.

I replied under my breath, "Please help," then said loudly, "How's Marta?" I had my back to the man with the red car, so he could not see my face or hand gestures.

I said to the man with the newspaper, "This man"—and I rolled my eyes in the direction of the man behind us—"this man . . ." but then I was at a loss. I didn't know the German word for *follow*. I repeated, "This man," and broke into English, "is following me." I then placed my left palm up and walked the index finger and the second finger of my right hand across my palm. The man leaned over, peered over his glasses, and stated in German, "I don't speak English." He then opened his newspaper and began to read. Of all the people in Berlin, I had to choose the one who did not speak English.

I was still panicking. This man was not planning on helping me. Should I continue with the ruse?

I leaned toward the man, pointed to an article, and stated, "This is interesting." I then whispered, "Can you please tell me if there is a man with black hair standing behind us."

The man sighed and looked over my shoulder. "No," he said. I sighed, leaned back, but did not dare look behind me. I thanked the man and continued to sit, nervously. The train came shortly thereafter, and I boarded behind the man with the newspaper. The man with the beautiful red car was nowhere in sight.

When I reached my stop, I jumped from the train and ran as fast as I could to the store. I was in luck—my friend Betsy was working. Betsy was from England and had lived in Berlin for many years. When I told her my story, she was sympathetic. She told me that she had to work for another four hours but informed me that I could stay at the store if I didn't feel safe. I stayed for a while but then decided to leave. The man with the beautiful red car had vanished, and I felt secure again.

"By the way," I said to Betsy, "what's the German word for *follow?*"

"Folgen," she said.

Another word to put on my Do Not Forget list.

A Schnauzer Named Collie

I could hear the phone ringing from my room. Should I answer it? Phone privileges had not been discussed, and I wasn't certain if my landlady would become angry if I answered. I was renting a room in a flat. My room was immediately across the hall from the phone.

The phone rang and rang. No one answered. I appeared to be the only one home. I took a risk and answered it myself. In my best phone voice, I said in German, "Schmidt residence."

The woman on the other end appeared to be taken aback as she didn't recognize my voice. She asked, "Who is this?" I identified myself. She then asked to speak to Mrs. Schmidt. I informed the woman that Mrs. Schmidt was not at home and took a message. I left the message by the phone.

A few hours later, there came a knock at my door. I answered it, and there stood Mrs. Schmidt. Mrs. Schmidt was a large woman in every sense of the word. She stood about six feet tall and easily weighed over two hundred pounds. She had shoulder-length blonde hair that was beginning to gray. Her cheeks were rosy, but her demeanor was not. A chain-smoker, Mrs. Schmidt's teeth and fingertips were yellow. Her voice was strained when she spoke, and she coughed repeatedly—and there she stood in my doorway, with her hands on her wide hips.

"Who is this?" she asked me as she thrust the message in my face.

"Affe," I replied.

"Who is Affe?" she asked.

"I don't know. She said her name was Affe," I told her.

"Affe," she chortled, "Affe? When did she call?"

"Oh, about two hours ago," I informed her.

"What did she want?" she asked me.

"I don't know. All she said was to tell you that Affe called," I replied.

Suddenly, Mrs. Schmidt burst into laughter. "Oh, Affe, my daughter!"

Mrs. Schmidt removed the message from my hand and wrote on it, speaking very slowly and underlying every letter, "E-v-a, my daughter!"

Both of us were in tears now. Confusing English with German, I had sounded out the woman's name as I had taken the message on the phone.

I had called the woman's daughter an ape.

No wonder Mrs. Schmidt was confused. No harm done though. I was a foreigner and had only been in Germany for two weeks. Mistakes were bound to happen.

The next day, Mrs. Schmidt asked me to buy some potatoes when I went to the grocery store.

"No problem," I told her. She gave me some money, and I purchased the potatoes. When I returned to the flat, Mrs. Schmidt was not home. I was greeted at the door by her schnauzer. His name was Collie. Now Collie was not a friendly schnauzer. At first, I thought he was aggressive toward me because he was not accustomed to me. But as the weeks and months wore on, he continued to growl and lunge toward me. I always attempted to place my key in the hole very quietly so he wouldn't hear me. Sometimes this worked, and other times it did not. Regardless, I would quickly shut the door behind me and race to my room before Collie could sink his teeth into me. This, I believe, became a game after a while. What else did Collie have to do but wait for me to return home?

So on this day, Collie was waiting for me at the door. He immediately began growling and snapping at me. Luckily, I had the bag of potatoes with me that I could use as a shield.

"Back, Collie!" I yelled at him. "No, Collie!" and lunged at him with the potatoes. He backed off momentarily but then came at me from behind. I swung around and lost grip of my own bag of groceries. The bag fell, and my groceries were strewn across the floor.

"Oh, so this is how you play!" I said to Collie.

I slowly leaned over as Collie continued to growl.

"Nice Collie. Nice Collie," I said. At the same time, I wondered if I would give this schnauzer an identity crisis my calling him a collie. The thought was fleeting, however, as I was in a crisis of my own.

I held the bag of potatoes firmly in my outstretched arms, creating a barrier between the dog and myself.

"Go ahead, bite the potatoes!" I said. "Yummy, yummy potatoes!" I taunted him. Collie turned around and walked away. I quickly picked up my groceries and left the bag of potatoes by the phone.

The next day, Mrs. Schmidt was knocking at my door again.

"What's this?" she asked, this time shoving the bag of potatoes in my face.

"Potatoes," I said. I suddenly felt guilty and wondered if Collie had somehow communicated to her that I had taunted him with the bag.

"These are new potatoes!" she exclaimed.

"New potatoes?" I asked.

"Yes, new potatoes! I didn't want new potatoes, I wanted old potatoes," she answered.

"I'm sorry if I bought you the wrong kind of potatoes. I don't know what new potatoes are. Back home, you go to the store and buy a bag of potatoes . . . ," I stammered.

"These are new potatoes. I wanted old potatoes. Potatoes not in a bag," she stated and walked away.

In spite of the communication problems that I was having with Mrs. Schmidt, she seemed to like me. When she went on vacation, she asked me to take over her hausfrau responsibilities. What this meant, basically, was that I was to sweep and wash the stairs in the hallway throughout the building. The building was four stories. I didn't mind it as it provided me with extra money.

As I was sweeping the steps leading to the second floor, a tenant approached me from above. She was an elderly woman and very friendly. She introduced herself to me and asked me what I was doing. I introduced myself to her and told her I was . . . uh-oh. What's the German word for sweeping? I didn't know what the word was, so I said, "I'm a little broom."

"Oh, how nice," the woman responded, and she continued down the stairs without another word.

Gerhard the Anchorman

I was twenty-three years old and working as a teacher's aide in a German/ American School in Berlin, West Germany. The year was 1981. I loved Berlin but hated my job. I was very lonely. I was shunned by Germans my own age for being an American, and I was loved by Germans twice my age for the same reason. "We will never forget what you Americans did for us during the war," the older Germans would say, while the younger Germans said, "You Americans are so egotistical. All you think of is, 'We're number one.' You don't know a thing about international affairs, and you don't demonstrate a desire to really learn about others."

Unfortunately, the younger Germans did have a point when it came to my knowledge of international affairs. Growing up in Michigan, I was pretty isolated from anything international—well, there was Canada, but that was different. Canada was just a short drive across the Detroit River. People spoke English in Windsor, and their main mode of transportation was by car. Canada did not seem like a foreign country to me; I wasn't familiar with its politics, and I certainly wasn't familiar with the politics of my own state. Yes, I hate to say it, but the younger Germans were right about me. Now that I've got that off my chest, I can tell you that I've vindicated myself as I've matured. I've become more politically aware and active and have taken the "Ignorant American" albatross from around my neck.

This particular evening in 1981, I was passing time at an Irish pub that I frequented often. I was there with my friend Susan, who also worked at the school.

We were doing our usual—standing at the bar, drinking Guinness, and talking to the blokes in the band. The only thing different was that Gerhard was there. Gerhard was also in his twenties, German, nice-looking, and employed as a newscaster, although neither Susan nor I had ever heard of him before. He claimed to have started doing the beat on the street, but he was so talented verbally that he quickly rose to the level of his current position as anchorman. His aspirations were to be a politician. He was studying political science at the local university. This was the first night I had met Gerhard. He was interesting and took a liking to me. He asked me out, and we had dinner the following Friday.

Dinner was pleasant, but I didn't feel any spark with Gerhard. We decided to go back to the pub and listen to the band. Once there, Gerhard became very quiet. I, on the other hand, blossomed. I joked with the band while they were on stage and let loose. Noticing Gerhard's demeanor, I turned to him and stated, "You're quiet all of a sudden."

Gerhard nodded and stated, "That's because I'm not allowed to talk as much as you."

"What do you mean?" I asked.

"One of my professors is a sorcerer," Gerhard explained. "He knows what I do for a living and doesn't think it's a good idea to strain my voice . . . so he put a spell on me . . . I can only speak ten thousand words per day. It's for my own good."

Intrigued, I pressed further, "How can you tell when you've gone over ten thousand words?"

"My mind is like a human computer," Gerhard explained. "I can tell when I'm approaching ten thousand," he stated, pointing to his head. "And if I go over, I become a deaf-mute."

"Oh my!" I exclaimed.

"It's for my own good," Gerhard repeated. "Really, it's nothing. If I approach ten thousand words in public, I just remain quiet. If I'm at home, I watch television."

I was soon to find out that talking was the least of Gerhard's problems.

"You know," Gerhard elaborated, "Napoleon could read a letter, write a letter, dictate a letter, and have a letter be dictated to him, all at the same time. I'm up to watching four television stations at the same time," he said proudly. "I have twelve televisions altogether. One day, I'll be able to watch all of them, on different channels, at the same time. Then I'll add radio stations. I have two radios right now."

For the life of me, I didn't know what to say. I just nodded and wondered what I had gotten myself into. More importantly, how was I going to get myself out of this date?! My mind raced as I tried to think of something clever. The band had in the meantime finished their set and approached our table. I spoke with the blokes, but Gerhard remained silent. *Maybe one of them could walk me home*, I thought. I turned my back slightly to Gerhard and rolled my eyes in his direction. The blokes just stared at me. I rolled my eyes again and mouthed the word *help*. No reaction. I mouthed the word in German, but still no reaction. They were too drunk and were quickly called away by the pub manager. My mind was still racing as they staggered away.

I stayed until the pub closed so that I was not alone when leaving with Gerhard. Gerhard walked me to the subway, and we parted ways. I never heard from Gerhard again—perhaps he had reached his ten thousand words. My roommate, on the other hand, was in dire need of a television set. She was an avid soccer fan, and the World Cup was fast approaching. She took it upon herself to contact Gerhard and inquire if he could spare a set. He eagerly complied with her request. They made arrangements for delivery while I made arrangements not to be home.

Sometimes I wonder about Gerhard today. Did he ever become the Napoleon of the 1980s? Did he ever become a politician? What happened to his professor?

Hmm, I wonder, what would happen if politicians today would become deaf-mutes—well, maybe not deaf, just mutes?

The Visit from Repo Man

My roommates in college were colorful characters. There was Beth, GiGi (affectionately known as Avocado by Beth), and Evie. All three of these girls knew each other from their hometown, a small rural community in our state.

GiGi was gregarious and down-to-earth. She had been an English major and moved with Beth and Evie for the adventure. Beth was also gregarious but somewhat snotty and manipulative. She came from a wealthy family and was accustomed to getting her own way.

Evie also came from a wealthy family and had attended charm school. Her family was always dressed to the hilt and would never consider going to the mall in jeans or washing their own laundry or ordering Chinese carryout, as I was soon to discover. Evie was very outspoken and a little gruff around the edges. Apparently, charm school didn't work for her. Evie was not attending school but, like GiGi, came along for the ride. She didn't like the other girls, and they didn't like her—they just needed another roommate for financial reasons. Actually, there had been a fourth girl from their hometown who had made the excursion to our campus; but she had graduated in December, found a job, and moved on. Thus the vacancy in the apartment for me. I had started the year living at home and commuting to school, but this quickly became tiresome.

GiGi and Beth shared a bedroom, while Evie and I shared the other. I related well with Evie, and she with me. It was soon that I discovered that she believed GiGi and Beth were lesbian lovers. I also discovered that she herself was cheating on her fiancé, who lived two hours away. Petey, as she referred to him, was of good stock. Her parents approved of him, and the marriage was cemented in stone. Petey was studying to be a veterinarian. He would be able to provide well for Evie. Poor Petey, however. Petey didn't have a clue that Evie wasn't in love with him, nor did he know that Evie was having an affair with a man twenty years her senior. To make matters worse, this man was married to a woman who was on dialysis. Her kidneys had failed one year earlier, and she began peritoneal dialysis while she waited on the transplant list. This meant that she dialyzed at home under very strict and sterile circumstances. A tube had been surgically implanted in her peritoneum, which allowed for the cleansing of her blood. A bag was attached at the end of the tube, outside of her body. She was required to change the fluid in the bag, which drained into the peritoneum, every six hours. This she did herself and, again, required very sterile circumstances. The slightest piece of dirt could cause infection and death. Unfortunately, she threatened noncompliance unless Evie's lover ended the affair. He refused to but did agree to move out. Evie, on the other hand, kept her mouth shut about any of this to Petey or to her family—she would be disowned and would lose her inheritance. I sympathized with her but had my own relationship difficulties to cope with. My boyfriend had not been accepted to the same university as I had and had moved to another state. The relationship didn't survive the year.

This particular day, GiGi was proofreading a paper for Beth, Beth was rubbing GiGi's shoulders, and Evie was off somewhere with her man. I was sitting on the sofa studying when the doorbell rang. GiGi jumped up and answered the door while Beth pouted. It was GiGi's friend Junkyard. Junkyard obtained his name by collecting garbage, extracting what he could and creating metal sculptures. He certainly was creative, but his work really was "junk." I don't know if he ever sold anything, but he appeared to be happy. Gigi greeted Junkyard and announced that they were on their way to see Repo Man. GiGi's friends always did have unusual names. GiGi herself was looking into changing her name to Intrigue. I wished them fun. Beth continued to pout. Just at that moment, Evie burst through the door. She was late! Petey and her family were expected any minute. She had to quickly shower and look her best.

Within five minutes, Evie's family arrived. Evie was still in the shower. Beth was pouting in her bedroom. I answered the door. I beckoned them in and told them Evie had been running late because she had done the laundry. Don't ask me where I came up with this lie; it just flowed from my lips. Her parents looked around the apartment, scouring it with their eyes. Evie's mother made a tsk noise, letting me know that she disapproved of something. Was it what I said, or did she come across a dust bunny in the corner?

"So tell me something about you," Evie's mother put to me. I told her that I was attending the university and felt the sweat begin to collect on my brow. Why did I feel like I was being scrutinized?

"Hmm," Evie's mother muttered. "And what do you do for fun?" I explained that fun was sometimes difficult to make time for while studying, but sometimes Evie and I would order in Chinese food and just talk and laugh.

Another "Hmm" from Evie's mother. Nothing from Evie's father or Petey. Just then, Evie entered the room with her hair wrapped in a towel.

Her mother immediately turned to Evie and said coldly, "Your roommate has been telling us that you've been washing clothes and ordering in Chinese food."

I've never seen the color vanish so quickly from someone's face before. Evie glanced at me while I shrugged my shoulders.

"Yes, sometimes," Evie blurted out.

"Hmm," her mother said again. "And where did you learn how to do the laundry . . . from the Chinese carryout?"

I was appalled at this comment but really didn't have time to react when the doorbell rang again. I was grateful for the distraction. I answered it, and there stood Evie's lover.

Perfect timing, I thought. I walked in the hallway and pulled the door behind me. I explained the situation to him and told him it was not a good idea to come in. Evie's lover told me that his wife's condition was worsening, and he didn't know what to do. He began to cry. I stood there, dumbfounded. With my hand still on the door behind me, I felt a tug which forced the release of the knob. There stood Petey. Well, the two men were finally face-to-face!

"I have to go to the car," Petey stammered.

I moved aside, letting him pass. Petey returned quickly and reentered the apartment, trying to avert our eyes.

I was still dumbfounded and just put my hand on the shoulder of Evie's lover. We stood like this for several minutes.

The door opened once again; this time Evie was face-to-face with her lover and me, followed by the rest of her family. Our minds quickly went into overdrive.

She blurted, "A lover's quarrel," to her family, while I stated, "This is GiGi's friend, Repo Man." Evie glared at me. I quickly recovered, stating, "GiGi and Repo Man are having some problems."

Evie stated, "Why don't you show Repo Man in? We're just leaving." I allowed Evie and her family to pass by before I led Evie's lover into the apartment. *Perfect timing*, I thought again.

I let Evie's lover cry a bit. He eventually gained his composure, then left, thanking me.

Shortly thereafter, GiGi returned home alone.

I stated, "Well, your friend Repo Man stopped by." GiGi gave me a puzzled look. I told her what happened.

She laughed and stated, "Well, I'm happy that Repo Man could be of service to you, but Repo Man is a movie. I don't have a friend by that name."

"Just as I said." I grinned. "Repo Man, the movie, was playing here tonight."

Lloyd

I was mildly obese in high school and painfully shy. At five feet four inches and close to two hundred pounds, I had very low self-regard. I had never been out on a date, nor had I ever been asked out on a date. Frankly, I don't know how I would have reacted if I had. Don't get me wrong—I wanted to be asked out, I longed to have a boyfriend—I just didn't have the self-confidence to be in a relationship.

So it was that I joined a weight loss program with a friend of mine at the end of the eleventh grade. I had no idea why she had joined; she was much thinner than I, and no one would have considered her overweight. I was just grateful that she began the program, thus prompting me to do the same. By the time I graduated from high school, I had lost fifty pounds and had started to feel more confident. Shortly before graduation, I began working at a small grocery store in a neighboring town. I was exposed to new people and was grateful to develop new friendships with people who didn't know my past, or that I was really painfully shy.

It was then that I met Lloyd. He was eighteen years old, tall, thin, and attractive. It was his fine features that attracted me the most to him: he had high cheekbones, a thin nose, thin lips, blonde hair, blue eyes, and a mustache. He was the opposite of what I was: a dumpy brunette. He was delicate but not effeminate. He was also gregarious, loud, and boisterous. I could always hear him singing or whistling from my vantage point at the cash register. He worked in produce.

Gregory also worked there. I was attracted to Gregory physically but soon became uncomfortable with his dialogue. Gregory could take the most innocent conversation and put a sexual spin on it. Potatoes were sexual, bread was sexual, milk was sexual—nothing passed Gregory's lips that wasn't sexual. I had never heard of sexual harassment before, nor would I have been able to stand up for myself even if I had.

Enter Knight in Shining Armour: Lloyd.

Oh, there is one thing I should mention about Lloyd. No one liked him. They all thought he had an opinion of himself that was elevated and that some of his stories were just that—stories. I didn't see these qualities in Lloyd however. I was grateful to have the attention of a boy and especially of one who came to my aid in fending off a sexual predator. Gregory, of course, didn't like the fact that Lloyd stood up for me, but he eventually backed off.

So it was, on my very last day in high school that Lloyd asked me out. I couldn't believe it! I finally got asked out! Thank goodness school was still in session—well, theoretically, albeit the very last day of my high school career. I didn't have to be ashamed anymore! I had been asked out on a date during high school!

I eagerly accepted Lloyd's invitation. We went out to the movies after work the following night. Don't ask me what we saw—I was too enthralled with the fact that I was on a date. After the movie, we talked in the parking lot and gazed at the stars. He told me about this constellation and that constellation, then pointed to no star in particular and stated, "See that star? That star is named after you—Beautiful Aureoles."

Then he kissed me.

Suddenly, the stars came plummeting down to earth, or maybe I was catapulted into space. All I knew was that I was in heaven. After all those miserable, lonely years in high school, I was finally in heaven!

Lloyd held me for a while, and then we said good night. We didn't make any plans to go out again, but it didn't matter because we would see each other at work. As luck would have it, my best friend would call me the next day and inquire if I was interested in going to a concert with her and her boyfriend. I told her all about Lloyd, and we made plans to double-date. Of course, I had to discuss it with Lloyd first. I couldn't wait to talk to Lloyd about it, and when I saw him, he immediately said yes. The concert was two weeks away, and although we didn't go out again during that time, it didn't matter to me. We were both fresh out of high school and had very little money. We had to save up to pay for the concert.

Lo and behold, the day before the concert arrived, my eldest sister presents me with a surprise—a letter she had found stuffed in the back door when she got up at 7:00 a.m. We lived on a small horse farm, and it was her turn to feed the horses. She found the letter as she opened the door to head toward the barn. By the time I had awakened and started my breakfast, she had completed her chores and was washing her breakfast dishes.

"This letter is for you," my sister said, handing me a blue onionskin envelope. "It looks like it's written in blood! It was stuffed in the door when I got up this morning."

I looked at the envelope in disbelief. Sure enough, it looked like it was written in blood. I had no idea who had addressed the envelope because there was no return name or address, and apparently, the writer had run out of blood because my first name was the only item that was scrawled on the envelope. I turned the envelope over and felt something thick inside, something other than a letter. I opened the envelope cautiously and peered inside.

The envelope contained a letter all right but also a small plastic bag. Inside the bag was a locket of blonde hair.

Still puzzled, I took the letter out and read its contents. The salutation and signature were written in blood, while the body of the letter was written in pen. Apparently, the writer was indeed short on blood. The letter read:

My Dearest,

I am sorry to tell you this, but I cannot go to the concert with you. My parents have once again pulled the strings, and I must stay home. I'm very sorry, but I know that you will understand. I'm writing this to you in blood because I'm Indian, and Indians always sacrifice for their squaws. I'm hoping that I don't faint before I am able to sign this letter. I know you will understand.

Forever,
Lloyd

From the look on my face, my sister could tell that something was wrong.

"What is it?" she asked.

I gave her the letter.
"Oh, weird," she commented. "You should dump him," she said and left the room. Always straight to the point, my sister was.

I sat there, dumbfounded. I didn't know what to think or say. I was angry that he told me the day before the concert and panicky about the cost of the ticket. Who would I find at this late date to replace him?

Now I felt like I was going to faint! I called up my best friend and told her the story. "Oh, weird," she said. No problem, however. She would ask her boyfriend's brother to come along. He was cute, she said, and would certainly be a good time.

I went to the concert and had an awful time. I wasn't attracted to this boy in the least and had to continuously fight off his groping hands. All I wanted to do was go home!

I didn't see Lloyd for almost two weeks. As fate would have it, we weren't scheduled to work together. My anger had subsided somewhat, but my feelings toward him romantically had changed drastically. I began to see him in a different light.

"So I got your letter," I said to Lloyd. Lloyd grinned. He had one hand behind his back and rocked from side to side. He ignored my comment and quickly pulled his hand out from behind him. In his hand was a small package wrapped in crumpled tissue paper.
"Forgive the wrapping job," he said. I looked at the gift and hesitated. "Go ahead," he said. "It won't bite!" I took the package from his hand and opened it slowly. Inside was a small silver and turquoise necklace in the shape of a phoenix. The chain was delicate, and I had difficulty opening the clasp. Lloyd helped me put it on.
"It's beautiful, Lloyd. Thank you," I said. I was slightly confused. I liked the necklace, but presenting me with this gift distracted me from my goal, which was to talk to him about his letter. If I didn't confront the issue now, I probably never would get the courage to again.

"Why did you write in blood?" I blurted out.

Lloyd pointed to my neck and said, "The necklace looks good on you."

"Thank you," I replied. I stared at him, waiting for a response.

"I thought you would understand how deeply I felt about you if I signed it in blood. It's the Cherokee way," Lloyd said.

"Cherokee? I didn't know you were Cherokee. Lloyd McFarley doesn't sound Cherokee," I responded.

"Well, I'm Cherokee on my mother's side. Her name is Squaw Pretty Face that Runs Like a Deer. Although in the Indian tradition the child takes on the mother's last name, my parents thought it would be easier to take on my father's name. Runs Like a Deer is too complicated," he explained. "So you like the necklace?"
He wanted to focus on the necklace while I wanted to find out more about his Indian heritage. Never having a boyfriend before, I was naive. Part of me wanted to believe him, but yet, this story . . .

"Did you notice the phoenix? Like the phoenix rising from the ashes, so too our love conquers all," Lloyd stated.

"What happened between you and your parents?" I asked.

"Oh, you know. This and that, that and this," he replied. Although Lloyd had told me a little about his family, he had never told me of any problems he was having with them. "The Indian way is to keep their young sequestered in their teepees, no reason given. I have to comply or chop all of my hair off," he explained.

Now let me remind you once again about Lloyd's features: very fine and delicate. He had short-cropped blonde hair. He had no hair to "chop off"!

"Did you get my locket of hair?" he quickly asked, as if this was something he could use to his advantage.

"Yes," I answered. "I didn't know what to do with it. Do you want it back?"

"No!" he exclaimed. "It's yours to keep! At first, I decided to protest, so cut some of my hair off . . . but then I decided to acquiesce," Lloyd said.

We were interrupted just then, and Lloyd had to return to the produce department.

The rest of the summer went by quickly, and our schedules rarely coincided anymore. We hadn't exchanged phone numbers because we would talk at work. The next time I went out with Lloyd was the week before I left for college. I told him that I thought it best to end our relationship since we were to be so far away. Lloyd agreed and stated that he would reluctantly "rope in that star" with my name on it—or maybe it was the star with his name on it—by that time, it didn't matter much to me.

It wasn't until Christmas break that I visited the grocery store again. Gregory was still working there, and Lloyd too. It was Lloyd's day off, but Gregory had a mouthful to say.

"I know you thought I was a pervert," he started, "but let me tell you the truth about Lloyd. Lloyd has a girlfriend who he's been dating ever since the tenth grade. They're talking about getting married."

I looked over at Joyce, who was standing next to Gregory. Joyce had been the other cashier and the only other woman employed in the store. She and I had had our girl talk during slow times.

Joyce nodded and added, "You know when you were supposed to go to the concert? He was at Cedar Point with his girlfriend . . . and you know that locket of hair he gave you—it was from his dog!"

I couldn't believe it. So that's where he got the necklace from, but how did he manage to smuggle it home without his girlfriend discovering it?

"Oh well," I stated. "That's in the past." And I stood there thinking about Lloyd's hair—hadn't I really seen a patch of hair missing from his scalp as he had turned away?

Stickbreaker

We were lucky to grow up in a neighborhood that had many children in it. Our house seemed to be the one where all the children congregated. We had active imaginations and were always making up games to play. I remember hiding behind the bushes in the front yard and yelling at the fruit vendor who was selling his wares from his truck.

"Strawberries! Get your fresh, rotten strawberries here!" I don't know if he ever saw us, but he never approached us or told us to stop. This we took as an invitation to continue. Our neighbors were not pleased. Especially Mrs. Mammamoose.

Mrs. Mammamoose was not her real name, of course; it was just a nickname that we had given her. She was a large Greek woman with a thick accent and a sharp tongue.

Mrs. Mammamoose didn't take too kindly when we played A Day at the Racetrack either. This game was my eldest sister's invention and required old tires and a good screaming voice. My parents had a collection of old tires that stood against the back wall of our garage. They used these tires as a buffer to protect the car in case they pulled up too closely to the wall. Obsessed with horses, my sister named all the tires and pretended the garage was a barn. So on racing day, we would take the horses out of the barn, line some of them on the bottom of the driveway, and keep the rest for racing. Two horses would race against each other to see who could get to the bottom of the driveway first. The race master would signal the start of the race. The jockeys would push the horses down the drive and loudly coax them on. Whoever was standing on the sideline yelled at the top of their lungs, hoping the horse they bet on would win. Someone also stood at the finish line to assure that none of the horses ran into the street. This was fun, but Mrs. Mammamoose did not see it that way. She complained to my mother that we were running the neighborhood down and making it look like a ghetto.

We continued playing.

There were two sets of siblings named Sally and Mary that lived in our neighborhood.

Sally and Mary R. lived around the block from us. They had the only swimming pool in the neighborhood. Their father was a policeman and worked the midnight shift. Their mother was a homemaker. Sally and Mary R. always seemed to get the latest toys and didn't seem to have much supervision. Sally and Mary R. would frequently stay up past midnight and come calling for us before 7:00 a.m. Back then, we didn't use doorbells but would literally stand on the porch and call out our friend's name in a singsong fashion until they came to the door. My mother would frequently yell out to Sally and Mary R. to go home and go back to sleep.

Sally and Mary H. lived across the street from us. I don't know what their parents did for a living, but I do remember that their mother once told me that I looked like Kim Novak. I didn't know who Kim Novak was so didn't know if this was a compliment or an insult. I was just happy that she didn't tell me I looked like Ethel Merman.

Mary H. was my middle sister's age. Both Mary H. and my sister were the leaders of the neighborhood and would periodically get into arguments that lead into full-fledged "wars." During these periods, people would choose which side they were on. I don't remember what triggered the last war, but everyone seemed to be against my sister. It was unfortunate that the issue couldn't be resolved before everyone moved (we all seemed to move around the same time)—relationships were severed, and bad feelings remained until the end.

I inadvertently started a war one time. It was a hot day; I was in a mischievous mood, and I became involved in a water-balloon fight. Instead of knowing when to stop, however, I landed a balloon on Timmy M. after most of the fighting had ended. He didn't take too kindly to this. He was all out of balloons so decided to go after me with the hose. He turned the faucet on and ran into the backyard to retrieve the end of the hose. Little did we know that my mother was in the backyard, taking down the dry laundry—well, what had been dry laundry until Timmy turned the water on! My mother was so upset; she complained to Timmy's mother. Timmy got in trouble and thought it unfair that he should suffer any consequences when I was to blame.

Sorry, Timmy.

Patty lived across the street from us, next to Sally and Mary H. She was a teenager and above associating with any of us. Patty had a boyfriend who drove a pickup truck. During the winter, he made a female snowman complete with breasts in the bed of his truck and drove around the neighborhood honking his horn. My mother asked him to move the truck when he parked it in front of our house one day.

The winter was one of my favorite times. We had a large backyard which we turned into a skating rink. One of my favorite activities was to go caroling with our church choir, then return to our house, drink hot chocolate, and go skating. I ran into a former choir member at a funeral last year, who told me that that was one of his favorite memories of childhood as well.

One year we had a large snowfall. I spent quite some time in the front yard making my own snowman. I was very proud of how large I had rolled the bottom snowball. I was just starting on the second snowball when our newspaperboy came walking by. He teased me and called me baby for making the snowman. I tried to ignore him, but I have to admit that his teasing got the best of me. I went inside to take a break; and when I came back out a little while later, my creation was destroyed, stomped to pieces. My mother was sympathetic and told me to make another snowman in the backyard. I don't know if she ever spoke to the paperboy about the incident. As luck would have it, she wouldn't need to.

The next summer, our paperboy made the mistake of breaking our prized stick. Now this stick was no ordinary stick. It was at least four feet long, thick, and very sturdy. We used that stick to make forts out of, to slay dragons with, and to measure distances with on our racetrack. We loved that stick.

One day, our paperboy decided to break the stick. Just like that, he approached my sister, grabbed the stick from her hand, and hit it against the tree! We were all enraged. Now my eldest sister was a tomboy and took great pride in asserting herself against the boys in the neighborhood. As soon as the first snap was heard, she raced over to our paperboy and jumped him. He ran away with a bloody nose and, soon thereafter, quit his paper route. Every now and then, I would see him in the neighborhood and would yell to him, "Hey, Stickbreaker! Heard you got beat up by a girl!" He would run the other way.

Now look who is queen of the neighborhood!

That's how Stickbreaker got his name. To this day, we fondly refer to him by this nickname. I don't know whatever happened to Stickbreaker, but my sister always catches a grin when she thinks back on the time that she beat Stickbreaker up.

As for us, we never were able to find another replacement stick of the same quality—odd to think that a stick could bring such joy to so many.

Homecoming

In 1972, my family and I moved to a small rural community. It had always been my mother's dream to have a horse farm, and her dream was finally being realized. Not a big horse farm, mind you, just ten acres and two horses to start.

The move itself was a nightmare. Our friends who lived down the street moved two days before we did. Since they had a baby, they asked my sister to babysit while they moved. My sister obliged but came down with the flu the next day. I came down with the flu on the day of our move. I don't remember much except sleeping and vomiting. My mother had kept me on a mattress in my bedroom. I was the last to leave our house in Detroit. My mother placed me on that same mattress on the floor of the sunroom in our new house, a room that had been added on.

At this point, it might be important for you to know that my parents purchased a home in a suburb of Detroit and moved it to our new property in "the sticks." I don't know much of the details except that this was no easy feat! I have been told that the house was moved in stages and that it had rested for several days on a corner which is now the home of a McDonald's. The reason that it is important for you to know this is that the contractors did a shoddy job of adding the sunroom, which caused the roof to leak when it rained. Unfortunately, we moved during the middle of a thaw in December. I remember feeling damp while lying on that mattress in the sunroom. I was too sick to care. On the bright side, I was too sick to lend a hand in any of the physical labor. The story goes that our movers were drunk, and the moving van got stuck in the mud in our front yard. Also, as the week progressed, the flu attacked my other family members. I don't remember how long I suffered; I only remember that my mother allowed me to open an early Christmas gift from my godparents: a matching scarf, hat, and mittens. I was too sick to appreciate them.

We all survived that traumatic move, although I don't know how my father managed! We lived on a dirt road—due to the thaw, the road was impassable. My father had to park his car three miles down the road, walk through the muck every morning, and then drive forty-five minutes to work! The scene was reversed, of course, after working a full day. He decided to quit smoking and got into good shape.

My Polish grandmother moved with us from Detroit. She had been renting an upstairs flat on the northwest side of town and was having difficulty making the rent. The flat had two bedrooms, and although she had no difficulty leasing the second bedroom out, she quickly discovered that it was not easy living with another person. She only leased the room once, to another elderly lady named Maxine. Now Maxine was spry and chipper and the life of the party. This in itself caused my grandmother to question the match, but she needed financial assistance, so she allowed Maxine to move in. Within a month, my grandmother started making such comments as, "I never see her use the facilities," or, "I never hear the water run in the bathroom." This we considered odd but brushed off—certainly, my grandmother was mistaken; everyone uses the facilities.

Everyone but Maxine. You see, the tenants in the lower flat were suddenly finding soiled rags in their backyard. They had no idea where the rags were coming from until one day—*bonk*, one landed on their son's head!

Maxine was asked to leave within the week.

When we moved, it only made sense that my grandmother would move with us too. Unfortunately, our new house was smaller than what we were accustomed to. With four bedrooms and one bath, quarters were tight. My grandmother had the bedroom off the kitchen. The back door was also located in the kitchen. Since the kitchen faced the barn, most of the traffic went through the back door—our front door was rarely used.

Homecoming night of my sophomore year had arrived. At our school, homecoming dance was not a formal occasion—the dance occurred immediately after the football game, and everyone attended wearing jeans and overcoats.

It was my first homecoming, and I had a lot of fun. So much fun that I didn't want to go home. I had a midnight curfew, so I had to watch the time. But kids will be kids; and whoops, wouldn't you know it, it was after midnight, and I was still at the dance!

I got a lift home from a friend of mine and asked her to drop me off on the road in order to avoid waking my parents. She obliged me. It was a crisp night. The moon was out and provided some light for me to find my way to the back door. While on the porch, I fumbled for my key. I had to perform this task delicately in order to remain undetected. I looked through the window and could see the dog sleeping nearby. If I were lucky, he wouldn't hear me. I stuck the key in the keyhole and turned it slowly. I grimaced when the lock clicked, anticipating the worst. The dog didn't move. I continued my motions, slowly turning the doorknob, then pushing on the door ever so slightly. Still no movement from the dog. OK, push a little bit more now, squeeze through the crack, and shut the door behind you quietly. This I accomplished with ease; but when I leaned against the door and let out a sigh of relief, the glass shattered, the dog began barking, and my grandmother screamed, "Lordy, Lordy, burglars!"

I yelled to my grandmother and to the dog, but it was too late—my mother was already at the door, baseball bat in hand.

"It's me, it's me!" I yelled. My mother put the bat down. I was busted.

My mother looked at the clock, then looked at me, then looked at the clock again.

"My, how time flies," I said. After midnight, my mother has no sense of humor.

"You're grounded," she told me. "And clean up this mess! We'll talk in the morning about how you will pay for all of this." My mother turned around and shuffled away with her baseball bat. What a pity that my father hadn't jumped from his sleep first—the consequences surely would have been more lenient.

The next day my mother informed me that I could not use the phone and would not receive my allowance for the next two weeks—of course, I still had to complete my chore but receive no payment for it. My chore was to muck the stalls. Not a glamorous chore but something that provided me with money.

So I grudgingly walked to the barn and began mucking the stalls. With every scoop of horse droppings, I complained to myself about how unfair the world was. How was I supposed to survive the next two weeks? How could I survive without talking to my friends after school? How could I continue to scoop the poop without getting reimbursed for it?

Through all my complaining, I happened to glance in the corner of the stall that I was cleaning. There was a small space where the kickboards met, and I noticed a stick protruding from it. I wondered how the stick happened to lie there and thought that it might be dangerous for the horse if I did not remove it. Still thinking about my unjust world, I leaned over and pulled on the stick. Much to my surprise, I discovered that it was not a stick at all . . . but the tail . . . of a very . . . dead . . . muskrat!

I immediately dropped the muskrat and ran from the barn screaming. I stood there shuddering and hyperventilating.

"I touched a muskrat . . . I touched a dead muskrat . . ."

Granted, I had gloves on, but still the thought of touching this gross dead animal gave me the creeps! What was I to do? I had to go back into the barn to dispose of the animal; I couldn't leave it lying in the middle of the stall. If I hadn't touched the carcass, it at least would have remained behind the kickboard—well at least most of it would have. Why did I try to pick it up?

No matter how I looked at it, I had to go back into the barn and face this hairy beast. I slowly approached the barn door and peeked inside. There was no movement. I took one step in and then another. I peered around the stall door and looked inside. There lay the pitchfork, exactly where I had dropped it. And there lay the muskrat, directly next to it. Luckily, the handle faced me instead of the kickboards, so I didn't have to walk over the muskrat in order to pick up the pitchfork. What was that? Did I see the muskrat move? What if it's not dead? I looked closely at its belly to see if it was moving. Was it my imagination, or was its chest moving ever so slowly?

I ran from the barn.

"OK, calm down," I told myself. Sweat was rolling down my forehead. I gained my composure and approached the barn door again, then the stall door. I peered inside. The muskrat had not moved. This time, I decided to move quickly; and in one fell swoop, I picked up the pitchfork, jammed it under the muskrat, whisked around, and ran from the barn screaming. I ran about fifty feet into the woods, then flung the pitchfork into the air. I hadn't intended on throwing the pitchfork; but in my haste to get rid of the dead beast, I lost grip of it, and it went flying. All the while, I screamed.

When the pitchfork landed, I stopped screaming, straightened my coat and my hair, and headed for the barn. It wasn't until I reached the barn that I realized that I had left the pitchfork in the woods. I turned right around, retrieved the pitchfork, and walked back to the barn. Who knows where the muskrat landed. I didn't want to know. I returned to my chore and swore that I would never get caught breaking curfew again.

That night at dinner, my sister told me that she had seen me running into the woods, screaming.

I told her that I had been practicing for a part in a play.

Salt-N-Pepper Shaker

I'm almost the girl David Sedaris refers to in *I Almost Saw This Girl Get Killed*—except the incident didn't happen in France; it happened in Michigan. It wasn't my shoe but my coat that fell from the carnival ride, and it didn't happen with my boyfriend; it happened with two other high school students. The reason I say two other high school students is that my version and my sister's version differ.

My version is that two of my friends were with me. Her version is that she and her friend were with me. Beyond that, I don't know what her version entails. I never wanted her to be the one who received all the glory when retelling the tale.

"You were what?!" I imagined others asking my sister. "You were stuck upside down on a carnival ride? How frightening!" And then I would imagine my sister going into every gory detail on how we were trapped upside down for thirty painstaking minutes, all the while keeping her audience in breathtaking suspense. Being the youngest in my family, I was accustomed to having my sisters take all the credit for the incredible incidents that took place in our lives. I was/am fed up with the lack of acknowledgement and was/am not willing to allow my sister to take credit for this amazing, death-defying incident.

So here's my version: It was a warm summer night in 1973. My sister had just graduated from high school and was spending her last summer at home before she left for college. I had just completed the tenth grade. Both of us were bored, so we decided to go to the town carnival. We lived in a small rural community that consisted mainly of horse farmers. The carnival was the biggest—and only—action for miles. We spent the first twenty minutes wandering the midway, escaping most of the money-losing entrapments. One attraction caught our eyes however. A man was beckoning us to throw tokens on various items. If the token landed on the item and remained there, we could keep the item. The man mainly had dishes that appeared to be cheap antique replicas. We thought this task relatively easy, so we purchased some tokens. I was surprised to find that I couldn't throw a token into a green vase that I had my eye on. After three attempts, I changed my object of desire to a brown plate. The plate had swirls on it that resembled a Celtic design. With one quick throw, my token landed on the plate. I jumped and screamed with delight. My sister also won a plate of similar design but of different color. We decided to keep the plates in the car so that we didn't have to lug them around with us. On our way to the car, I ran into two of my friends while she ran into one of hers.

While securing the plates in the car, we decided to go our separate ways. We would meet again at the car at 10:30 p.m.

My friends and I wandered back to the action, talking about boys and whether we would get our sisters' rooms when they left for college.

Our wandering ended in front of the Salt-N-Pepper Shaker, a ride that looked like the grasshopper oil drills you commonly see in Texas. The difference, however, was that there were "heads" on both ends of the beam that lifted you into the air—while one "head" was in the air, the other was near the ground, and so forth, continuously swinging up and down. The "heads" were also not stationary but could be manipulated to swing by the distribution of your weight. Somehow, however, the "head" would always face down during its return journey to the ground. This created the illusion that you were about to crash into the earth, face-first.

So it was on this warm summer night that my friends and I decided to take a chance on the Salt-N-Pepper Shaker. The "head" swung back and forth as the three of us climbed on board. We were secured into our seat by a metal bar that came down on our laps. We were then enclosed by a wire mesh that came down over our heads. I, luckily, was the last one in, so sat to the left, by the door. My two friends sat to the right of me. We slowly made our ascent to the top and then stopped with a lurch while the other "head" was being loaded. During this time, we were devising a plan on how to control the ride—would it be safer to keep our bodies still, or would it be to our benefit to redistribute our weight in order to obtain full movement of the "head"? We all agreed to keep our bodies still. Unfortunately, we quickly discovered that this was an impossible feat. Gravity took over, and we had no control over the swaying vehicle.

Cycle 1 was completed slowly and resulted only in a few grunts by the three of us. During cycle 2, momentum was building. Cycle 3 was faster yet, and at this point, we began to scream. Cycle 4 ended abruptly during the middle of our downward thrust. Our heads were thrown back, and I remember hearing a cracking sound when my friend's head hit the back of the compartment.

"Ow," I heard her say, or was it me that I was hearing? I really couldn't tell at that time because I was mortified with the sight that lay in front of me. The vehicle stopped midway between apex and ground. We were stuck in midair, facing the earth. This is where my position in the compartment was important—the wire mesh curved around the vehicle and closed by the door. I could easily hold on to the mesh. So could my friend on the farthest side. My friend in the middle, however, had no mesh to hold on to as the mesh curved away from her. She had nothing solid to hang on to and had no other recourse but to dig her nails into my flesh.

"Ow!" I cried—this time I was certain it was me.

"Get your claws out of me!" As I struggled to remove her nails from my arm, my coat, which had been gently tied around my shoulders, became loose and fell toward the mesh. I let go of my friend's fingers and grabbed for the coat. It was a flimsy, lightweight nylon windbreaker that could easily fit through the crack between the mesh and the bottom portion of the compartment where we were seated. When I let go of my friend's hand, she dug her nails even further into me. "Ow!" I cried again, "Get off!" I once more grabbed my friend's hand but, in so doing, lost grasp of my coat. I saw it fall to the ground in slow motion. Since I hadn't reached the age where I started swearing yet, the most I could muster was, "Darn. There goes my coat!"

The coat landed without a sound and stayed there only briefly before a boy of about seven or eight picked it up. He then looked up at our compartment and proceeded to run off with it. "Hey, that's my coat!" I yelled as I pounded the mesh.

"What are you doing!" my friends yelled at me. "Are you trying to get us killed? Don't rock us!"

So there we sat, in the air, facing downward with our legs bracing the front of the compartment, our fingers clenching the wire mesh and my middle friend frantically gouging my arm out.

It took us a while to calm down. Does anyone know we're up here? The incident wasn't attracting a crowd, and after ten minutes of nonaction, we began to scream. To no avail. No one responded to us. No one tried to calm us down or let us know that help was on the way. No one knew we were alive!

OK. So maybe it is better to rock the thing! We tried to redistribute our weight and decided to lean forward on the count of three. We knew this might mean that we would be stuck on our heads, but we were willing to take the risk.

OK. On the count of three . . . one, two, three. We leaned forward quickly. I remember grunting while my middle friend screamed. We returned to our original positions swiftly. Nothing happened.

So now what? Let's try it again.

One . . . two . . . three . . . nothing. One more time. Still nothing.

A good fifteen minutes had passed by that time, and our muscles were getting sore from the strain of bracing ourselves. Had we given up our vigil, we could have landed against the wire mesh like rag dolls—with the exception that the metal bar across our laps was holding us in place—but when you're in midair, staring at the earth, you don't think of these things. In fact, I believe that my lap became numb from the pressure of the bar, so I couldn't feel it holding me anyway. All I could think of was, *Just exactly how does it feel to smash your face into the ground? What will my funeral be like? Will my sisters cry?*

It wasn't for another fifteen minutes that the machine lurched forward and completed its descent. Although our limbs were sore, we were still able to scramble out of our compartment and straighten our clothing. The ride operator said nothing to us, no apologies, no explanations. We were all relieved that the horror was over. Instead of owning the fear, however, I heard one of us say, "What a stupid ride!"

Yes, indeed, that ride was ignorant.

When we returned to the car, I told my sister about the event. "Oh, so that was you," she said calmly. What—didn't she hear me?! I could have died!

So that's my story, and I'm sticking to it.

Rolling a Drunk

I sat in the backseat of the 1972 Ford with my head leaning against the window. The pane was cold and damp, but I kept my head in the same position out of fatigue. The year was 1984, and I was visiting my boyfriend John. He was attending a university in Illinois and had difficulty getting over the fact that he had not been accepted into graduate school at the University of Michigan while I had. You see, John was a genius, or at least that's what he thought, and I was not. Instead of the University of Michigan, John was accepted into a university in Illinois and was studying clinical psychology. His best friend Jack lived in Chicago, which was a stone's throw away. John met Jack while both were undergraduates studying psychology at the University of Michigan. Their personalities were diametrically opposite. John was introverted, while Jack was extroverted. John was awkward around women, while Jack was quite comfortable. John only had one previous girlfriend before dating me, while Jack gave the impression he had dated extensively. I never knew the truth about Jack's dating history, but I could understand why a girl would be attracted to him yet repelled. Jack was tall, dark, and handsome but was very narcissistic. Whenever Jack spoke of an ex-girlfriend, John would roll his eyes. I found this quite funny as both boys desired to be the other. In fact, they often switched names and attempted to change their personae.

So it was on this chilly night in November that I found myself in the backseat of John's car listening to John and Jack chatter about the girls in Chicago. It was a very stressful period of my life, attending graduate school and attempting to keep the relationship with John alive. We had dated for approximately six months before he left for Illinois. Although I knew exactly where my feelings stood, I was not certain about John's. I would periodically find love poetry written by John that was not written for me. He would deny that it meant anything, that he was just writing lyrics, and that I should just chill out. John hoped to someday be a famous songwriter should clinical psychologist not pan out. We were six hours away by car. I visited on the weekends when I could, and this particular weekend we decided to meet up with Jack in Chicago. One of Jack's friends was moving from a cockroach-infested apartment to another apartment across town. John had volunteered to help move Jack's friend with his 1972 Ford. It should be pointed out that John's car was fourteen years old at the time and had previously belonged to the sheriff's department in a small Michigan town. Although someone had done their best to remove the sheriff insignia from the sides of the car, it was still quite obvious that the car had been some type of police car by its markings. Mainly white, the car still had a black circle on both the driver's and front passenger's doors.

Jack was giving John directions to his friend's house when he suddenly realized that he was lost. He instructed John to turn into a parking lot of an abandoned strip mall in order to gather his thoughts. Jack declared that fate had brought us to this location for some reason, and the reason would come to him if he could just meditate for a moment. Jack was living with his parents and was extremely depressed. He was not attending school and was trying to determine what to do with his life. Living with his parents wasn't helping as they frequently pressured him to make a decision. Jack decided to spend two weeks in a monastery to sort things out.

"People do this all the time," Jack told us. "It's cool, the hip thing to do. I'll spend two weeks meditating and communing with nature. I know I'll be led in the right direction," Jack explained.

"Are you planning on shaving your head and wearing a robe too? And no women?" John asked.

"I can handle it," Jack replied. "Hey, look over there!" Jack pointed to the far end of the parking lot. I strained my eyes to see what Jack was excited about. There, among the weeds and litter, lay a man with his face down. His clothes were dirty and disheveled. He lifted his head and mumbled, then bellowed out something undecipherable, which I interpreted as singing.

"Let's roll him!" Jack said. I didn't quite understand what Jack meant, but I could tell by the tone of his voice that it was not something good. "Yeah, let's roll him," he repeated. "I can see the headlines, 'Drunk Rolled by Psychology and Social Work Graduate Students.'" This was another indication that Jack was up to no good—why was he leaving himself out of the equation? My anxiety increased when John agreed to the suggestion.

"Why not," he said. "We have nothing better to do, we're lost, and I need some excitement in my life."

I began to perspire. Jack was the ringleader in their relationship, and I was worried that he would really be able to influence John in completing this crime.

Jack said, "Yeah, I need some excitement in my life, too . . . and I need something to contemplate at the monastery. Here's what we'll do. Monica, you go out first and talk to the guy. You know, assess just how incapacitated he is. We'll wait in the car until you come back. If he's really a goner, we'll go out—John, you roll him over, and I'll go through his pockets. Monica, you will take over the driver's seat—I'll tell you where to go, don't worry."

Don't worry?! I was worried plenty! First of all, why me? Why did I have to initiate this plot? How did I know that they wouldn't take off on me when I was out of the car? My relationship was souring with John. How did I know that he wouldn't see this as an opportunity to ditch me? Second, what if the drunk was dangerous, albeit at this point he appeared to be quite harmless. What if he was injured? What if he needed our help? On the other hand, if I got in the driver's seat, I could ditch them; but then again, I was in a strange city late at night and totally lost. No, this was not a good idea. *Why are we—I mean you—plotting to commit a crime?!*

"I don't think this is a good idea," I said. "Rolling a drunk is a crime in Michigan, and I have very high standards to live up to. I'm a graduate student at the University of Michigan, you know!"

"Yeah, right. Ms. Snob," Jack replied.

"I think the better idea is to see if he needs our help," I said. "Yeah," Jack answered, "You go see if he's OK, and we'll roll him!"

I responded with something about having compassion for others, and the conversation quickly turned into a debate about whether men are inherently evil. John apparently became impatient with the discussion, quickly threw the car in reverse, and sped out of the parking lot, wheels squealing. I thought there was something ironic about a crime being plotted in a former sheriff's car.

Well, that's the closest I've ever come to rolling a drunk. To this day, I don't know if John and Jack were seriously considering committing this crime. When I spoke to John about it afterward, he brushed it off as something frivolous. I never saw Jack again, but I truly believed that he had been depressed enough to commit this act—and bring us along with him.

I can see the headlines now, "Drunk Rolled by Psychology Graduate Student and Would-be Monk." The article would read, "Social work graduate student had her wits about her and proved that she indeed was the genius of the group."

The Shopping Mall

I was sitting at a four-way stop sign the other day waiting for my turn to proceed. After several minutes of waiting, I asked myself, "When will this light turn green?" I was awakened from this train of thought when another car approached me from the opposite direction, stopped briefly, and then proceeded on. It suddenly hit me that I was sitting at a four-way stop sign, not a four-way stoplight.

The next day, I happened to glance at my calendar and realized that the contractors were supposed to install my new windows the following day. It was 3:30 p.m., and they had not called yet to inform me of the time that they were planning on working at my house. I knew that they only answered their phones until 4:00 p.m., so I took it upon myself to call them up. While the secretary put me on hold, I reviewed all the errands and important items on my to-do list that I had yet to accomplish. The secretary came back on the phone and gave me a time frame. *Good,* I thought, *I'll still have time to go running and beat the afternoon heat after they leave.* It wasn't until I was relaxing several hours later in front of the TV when I realized that it was only Thursday, not Friday, and the contractors were not scheduled to install my windows until Saturday.

"Oh no," I worried. "What if I forget that tomorrow is not Saturday and I mistakenly miss work?" I immediately jumped up from the sofa, ran into my bedroom, and set my alarm. The last thing I needed to do was to get reprimanded for missing work! The next day, I was awakened by my alarm, and I went to work tired but there in body nonetheless. I walked to my office and stuck the key in the door. I turned the key, but the lock jammed. No matter how hard I tried to turn the key, it wouldn't budge. *What a great way to start the day,* I thought. I walked down to a coworker's office and asked to borrow her WD-40. I returned to my office, sprayed the lock, and placed the key once again inside. It was at that point that I realized that I was attempting to open my office door with the wrong key.

I'm stressed-out. The signs are everywhere that I need a break, but I don't have time to take one. Although I've experienced other stressful times in my life since then, I'm reminded of my time in graduate school. I was totally and completely stressed-out with attempting to manage my coursework, my internship responsibilities, and my love life. It seemed as if I was being pressured in all areas, and there was no way out.

So one day, I decided to take a break and visit my grandmother. "How's school going?" my grandmother asked me.

"Fine," I stated. "We just received our report cards, and I got all As," I said proudly.

Without a blink, my grandmother stated, "Your oldest sister is a genius, you know."

What?

Didn't she hear what I just said? I'm the one in graduate school, and I'm the one who received all As. You didn't see my sister attending graduate school!

I changed the subject. "So do you want anything from the grocery store?" I asked.

"Yes. Can you get me those shortbread cookies that I like so much—you know the ones, the square ones," she said.

I confirmed that I knew indeed which cookies she wanted and ran to the store. Anything to get away from being compared to my sister. When I got to the store, however, they were all out of square cookies. I bought the round cookies and returned to my grandmother's apartment.

"Oh no," she said. "These won't do. I said the square ones, not the round ones."

"They didn't have the square ones," I explained.

My grandmother shook her head and repeated, "These won't do. These are round, not square."

I rolled my eyes and stifled a scream. I changed the subject again. Maybe my grandmother needs a change of scenery. Maybe she would like to go to the mall!

"Grandma, would you like to go for a ride? Do you want to go to the mall?" I asked.

"I don't know," she responded, "It's too big."

"You don't have to walk around, I can get you a wheelchair," I said.

"Oh heavens, no!" my grandmother replied. "I'll walk, thank you!"

A word about my grandmother: she weighed over two hundred pounds and had severe arthritis in her knees. She was bowlegged and walked with not one, but two canes. Walking any great distance was difficult for her, and I knew that she would not survive in the mall without a wheelchair.

Another thing about my grandmother: she was a stubborn Polish woman.

We arrived at the mall and immediately began to argue over whether she required a wheelchair. My grandmother's voice began to get quite loud as she insisted that she did not require one. I was beginning to get embarrassed, so I backed down. My grandmother wanted to visit a particular shoe store that was on the first level, so we took the elevator down. By the time we reached the shoe store, my grandmother was spent. She insisted on going home immediately although we had not yet perused the store. I wasn't planning on arguing with her, so I agreed. The problem was that we were nowhere near the elevator. In fact, we were equidistant between the elevator, the escalator, and the stairs. My grandmother was terrified of the escalator, so that option was quickly ruled out. My grandmother chose to take the stairs. Unfortunately, here's what her plan was: we would walk to the stairs; then she would get down on her hands and knees, and I would push her up the one hundred or so steps.

If I could have laughed, I would have done so, but I was so frustrated with this stubborn Polish woman that it never crossed my mind.

"No, Grandma, I can't do that! It's too dangerous, both for you and for me. What if I can't push you? And do you know how embarrassing it will be? Do you really think that I can push you up those stairs without people laughing at us?"

My grandmother sneered at me and walked in the direction of the stairs. I ran behind her, talking to her sternly beneath my breath. It was to no avail. We reached the bottom of the stairs.

"OK," she said, "I'll get down on my hands and knees, and you push me up!"

I crossed my arms and looked at the stairs. "Grandma, look how thin those steps are. How do you plan on kneeling on them? And, Grandma, I'm sorry for being so blunt, but you have arthritis in your knees—how do you plan on even bending over?" She knew I had a point.

"Oh hush!" she said. "Just do what I say! I'm your grandmother!"

I didn't budge. "Sorry, Grandma, but I can't do this," I snapped. I was beginning to worry that my grandmother was really planning on throwing herself onto the stairs—and then what would I do? There was no way that I could push my two-hundred-pound grandmother up the stairs, and there was no way that I would ever be able to show my face in the mall again!

Suddenly, a man appeared from nowhere.

"Can I be of assistance?" he asked. I glared at my grandmother as I explained the situation to the man.

"Let me help you," he said to my grandmother. Before my grandmother could protest, the man grabbed her under her arm and whisked her up the stairs. I was left at the bottom of the stairs holding her canes but could hear her quite clearly proclaiming that he was an "angel sent from heaven" all the way up the steps. The man left my grandmother at the top of the stairs.

When I caught up to her, she spewed, "If your sister had been here, she would have known what to do!"

And so it goes when you're surrounded by geniuses.

I need a break. Maybe I'll go to the mall.

Crossed Hands

Every summer, the people of southeast Michigan go bonkers over classic cars. Apparently, cruising Woodward Avenue and possibly doing a little bit of drag racing was popular during the '50s and '60s. What started out as a small group of nostalgia seekers in the '90s has turned into a behemoth megainvasion of classic car junkies from all across the world.

Every summer, sixteen miles of Woodward Avenue, from Ferndale to Pontiac, is assaulted mainly by baby boomers who want to relive their past. They spend months polishing their cars and begin their attack of the area weeks before the official cruise. The day of the cruise, participants drive up and down the avenue while spectators sit in their lawn chairs on the sidewalk. Both participants and spectators dress up in '50s and '60s clothing. Some dress up as Elvis; others wear poodle skirts. I try to avoid the area.

The news reported that the event attracted over one million spectators and thirty thousand cars this year. This year was special as it was also the two hundredth anniversary of Woodward Avenue, a route that was once the only means for north/south travel from Detroit to the northern suburbs. As a result, a Hands Across Woodward was planned. This event was similar to the Hands Across America event that took place in the '80s. If you recall, people all over the United States congregated on a certain day, at a certain time, and held hands. This was to promote peace and unity across the country. In the Woodward event, people were asked to begin their human chain in downtown Detroit. The chain was to extend to the city of Pontiac, along Woodward Avenue. I did not attend the event, and I don't know how successful it was, although I did see some pictures of it on the news. I had attended the original Hands Across America, and that experience had been enough for me.

I was fresh out of graduate school in 1986 and working my first job as a social worker in a hospital in Indiana. Coming from Ann Arbor and moving to a small conservative city was a challenge, to say the least, but I was up for the challenge. Sometime after moving to Indiana, the buzz was brewing about Hands Across America. I was certainly interested in participating, but my fellow social workers were not.

"Ew," they said. "What if we get AIDS?"

Luckily, a friend of mine from Ann Arbor was interested in traveling to Indiana to participate. The event came and went, and thereafter, I was jokingly referred to as the social worker who touched a stranger's hand. I jokingly referred to my coworkers as fork and knife fanatics as they always ate their fruit with a fork and knife.

In 1987, I received word from my parents that my grandmother was in failing health. She was not expected to survive the week. I had to quickly drop everything and speed back to Michigan. Because I was in such haste, I did not cancel my newspaper delivery. Instead, I asked a friend, a fellow social worker, to come over to my apartment, take in the paper, and water my plants.

She said, and I quote, "No problem."

I arrived in Michigan on a Friday. My grandmother died the next day. I was away from Indiana a total of seven days. Upon my return, I found seven newspapers stacked at my front door and three wilted plants inside. I thought perhaps that an emergency had befallen my friend; but when I spoke to her about her absence, she merely stated, "I didn't feel like coming over."

And so began my exodus from Indiana.

So now I am back in Michigan, where I truly feel at home. I learned a lot during my stay in Indiana. I am now very proficient at eating cantaloupe with a knife and fork! I do not mean to sound sarcastic—this is a very good skill to possess. It certainly makes eating cantaloupe a lot less messy!

Alex

This is the story of another genius: Alex, the incredible bilingual dog.

Alex was not a good-looking dog. At first glance, Alex looked like a German shepherd. From afar, Alex looked like a corgi. He had big ears, a round belly, and stubby legs. His markings were black and tan with a patch of white on his chest. His right front paw was also white with a smattering of tan spots. Too short to be a German shepherd and too tall to be a corgi, I told everyone that he was a combination of both. I really didn't know what his lineage was because he was a stray. I only knew that the minute I saw his big brown eyes, I fell in love with him.

Alex and I met on a cold day in March. The forecast called for a snowstorm to move in that night. It was cloudy and the perfect day to expect snow. I arrived at work at my normal time, and as I walked to the building, I was greeted by a very friendly dog. He seemed to be happy to see me as he came running up from behind me, his entire body wiggling to and fro, ostensibly propelled by his tail.

"Well, hello there, little fella!" I said to him. I leaned over and petted him. I noticed that he did not wear a collar. He sat down and raised his paw. I grabbed it and shook it.

"Pleased to meet you," I said, "My name is Monica. Who are you?" He just looked at me with his big brown eyes. I examined his paws and noticed that the pads of his feet were soft. Had the pads of his feet been rough, I would have guessed that he had been roaming the streets for a while. Wherever he came from, he hadn't been on the street very long.

"Well, I have to go to work. I'll see you later," I said to the dog. When I entered the building, I asked my coworkers if they knew who the dog belonged to. No one did, but everyone agreed that he was very friendly. I went about my business for the rest of the day and forgot about the dog that had greeted me in the morning.

I walked wearily to my car at the end of the day. I was tired and ready to relax at home. I was aware of the storm that was coming and wanted to just sip some hot chocolate and read a good book. As I turned the corner and approached my car, I saw him. There he was, lying on the ground next to my front door. The minute he saw me, he jumped up and began wagging his tail again.

"Oh, it's you!" I said in surprise. "What are you still doing here? Don't you want to go home?" He pranced around me in circles and wiggled his way in between my legs. "You are so cute!" I said. "Where's your home?" He ignored me and continued to wiggle his way in between, through, and around me. I leaned over and petted him. "What am I going to do with you?" I asked. I lived in an upstairs flat, and pets were not allowed. "Wait here. Let me try one more time to see if I can find your master." I returned inside and asked the remaining coworkers if they knew anything about the dog. No one did.

I didn't know what to do. I knew the storm was coming, and I knew the parking lot would be empty soon. What would happen to this dog? Would he survive the storm? Where would he go? How would he eat? Would he freeze? I had to do something.

At that point, the security guard said to me, "Take him home."

Take him home? How could I?

"Take him home," he repeated. "I'll help you get him in your car."

"OK," I said.

I couldn't believe what I just said, but in a blink of an eye, I made what I thought was a life-or-death decision.

We walked out to the car, and there he was, lying right next to the driver's door. He lifted his head and greeted us again. I fumbled with my keys. Was I doing the right thing? What would his real family feel? Would they worry about him? Would they miss him? I was deep in thought when suddenly I realized that the security guard was backing away.

"What's the matter?" I asked.

"I'm afraid of German shepherds," he said.

"Well, he's a real friendly dog, see?" I said. The guard had his back plastered against the truck that was parked next to my car. "Yeah, I see," he said with a trembling voice.

I hadn't planned on this. My thoughts were racing as I unlocked the car.

"I can do this," the guard said. "I can do this."

"OK," I replied, "I'll open the back door, and let's see if he just jumps in."

Wishful thinking. Thirty minutes later, after lifting and pushing and shoving, the friendly dog was finally secure in my backseat. I turned to thank the security guard, but he was long gone. I could see him wipe the sweat from his brow as he ran back to the building. I yelled to him, but he didn't turn around.

I drove home slowly as I was not accustomed to driving with a dog in my car. The dog whined and paced the entire time—apparently, he was not accustomed to riding in a car either. When I got home, I ran inside looking for something to use as a leash. I didn't want to leave him alone in my car for too long for fear he would tear the car up. I grabbed some scarves and tied them together as I ran back outside. I opened the back door and loosely tied the scarves around the dog's neck.

Then I waited.

I didn't know what I was expecting, but I guess I thought the dog would be only too happy to leave the confines of the car. The dog plopped down and dug his heels in. I tugged on the scarves, and they slid off the dog's neck. I retied them and tried again. They came undone. I tried one last time and made certain the scarves were secure. I pulled, but the dog would not budge. I decided to push from behind, risking the possibility that the dog would run away once he was free of the car. I pushed, and the dog jumped from the car. Then he plopped down and remained there for thirty minutes. No matter how I coaxed, the dog would not move. My patience was running thin.

"OK, dog," I said, "you leave me no other alternative but to pick you up and carry you!" I really didn't know how much the dog weighed but guessed that he weighed at least fifty pounds. I didn't know if I could carry a traumatized fifty-pound dog across the lawn, up the porch stairs, and into the stairwell of my apartment; but I had no other choice.

I leaned over and gave the dog a blow-by-blow account of what I intended on doing. "OK. I'm lifting you up now," I said. The dog was heavy. He squirmed in my arms, and I was afraid that I would drop him. I took two steps and repositioned him in my arms. He whined. I walked as fast as I could to the porch and walked up the steps with uncertainty.

"My back," I complained. I set the dog down by the door and opened it. "Go ahead," I said to him. I gently pushed him with my legs, and the dog finally moved on his own accord.

I shut the door behind me and eyed the fifteen steps that lead to my flat.

"This is where I stop," I told the dog. "You will have to find your own way up these steps!" There was no door separating the stairwell from my apartment, so the dog could easily enter on his own accord. I petted the dog and went upstairs.

The dog remained at the bottom of the stairs for two days. On the third day, when I came home from work, I found him standing at the top of the stairs, wagging his tail and carrying one of my socks in his mouth.

Fast-forward three years, and I am now living in my own house. I have also acquired a kitten that had been born in my sister's barn. I have named the dog Alex, and the kitten Binky. Alex and I like to take long walks in the woods nearby. Although there is a path in the woods, I allow Alex to roam free. For some particular reason, Alex never does his "business" on the path but will run into the bushes and return when he is finished. Alex also enjoys playing fetch. I have taught him the German word for *fetch* and for *stick*. This particular day, Alex and I are playing fetch in the woods. I have found a sturdy stick that is the right size for Alex that won't break when he bites into it. Alex taunts me with the stick, running up to me, then quickly running away when I grab for it. Suddenly, he leaves the path and enters the bushes. He returns after a brief time, without the stick.

I ask him in German, "Where's the stick?" Alex immediately runs back into the bushes, returns with the stick, and the taunting continues.

Wow, I think. *What a brilliant dog!*

Later that night, Binky becomes obsessed with scratching the patio door as my boyfriend and I are watching TV. Alex is lying at my feet. I yell at Binky, but she does not stop scratching the door. I yell at her again, but you know, cats will be cats and just can't figure out when someone is addressing them. I'm getting frustrated, but I'm too lazy to get off the couch. Alex lifts his head and looks at me. I look back at him and say, "Alex, go over to Binky and tell her to stop doing that!"

Loyal dog that he is, Alex jumps up, runs to the door, and nudges Binky with his nose. Binky then stops scratching the door and walks away. Alex returns to his place by my feet. My boyfriend and I are speechless.

What a brilliant dog.

Chocolate Milk

About the same time that I met Alex, I was having stomach problems. This was nothing new to me. I first started having problems as an undergraduate. I was treated for an ulcer then but later found out that I never had an ulcer. In the meantime, my stomach would give me periodic problems, and I would treat it with chocolate milk. Regular milk probably would have sufficed, but I really didn't like the taste of plain milk unless it was in cereal or with cookies.

So on this particular day, I was at work and having stomach pains. I decided to walk to the small convenience store that was across the street. The store had been part of a gas station at one time. Although the gasoline was long gone, the empty pumps remained. I had never been in the store before but was hopeful that they had milk as there was not another store around for miles.

I opened the door and entered. The store was dark, and it took my eyes a moment to adjust. Just one room, I could see a dairy case approximately twenty feet from the door. To the right was a counter enclosed in glass. A small hole was cut into the glass, which was used for communication purposes between store clerk and customer. A drawer was located beneath the hole, similar to those one would find at a bank drive-through, to exchange money and convenience items. Behind the counter stood the lone employee of the store, a slight woman, not much taller than myself. Two women stood in front of the counter near the dairy case. A Hispanic man stood closest to the door with his back to me. The two women turned to me as I entered the store. I smiled at them, they nodded at me, and I walked toward the dairy case. The Hispanic man did not move. As I pulled on the door to the case, the man said, "A white woman just walked in here."

I was surprised that he had identified me as a white woman since he had not turned around. I ignored him and pulled on the door. The door wouldn't budge. The salesclerk told me that the doors were locked and that I had to let her know what I would like to purchase—she would then retrieve them and slide them through the drawer.

"Oh," I said and walked toward the counter.

"A white woman is in here," the man spewed.

"I'd like a pint of chocolate milk please," I told the saleswoman. I stood next to the man, well, basically because there was no place else to stand. He reeked of alcohol and teetered from side to side. I thought he was harmless, although I have to admit that my guard was up.

"What's a white woman doing in here?" he asked sharply. "Getting chocolate milk," I responded.

"I bet you're afraid of me, aren't you?" the man asked me. The woman who was standing closest to my left quickly came to my defense and stated, "Hell, I'd be afraid of you too considering the condition you're in!" I turned to the woman and smiled while the rest of the women laughed. The man did not laugh however. Instead, he smirked and said under his breath, "Huh! White woman!" I turned to the man and noticed that the whites of his eyes were not white at all, but yellow. I wondered if he was in liver failure.

"Look," I said, "I'm just getting some chocolate milk."

"Leave her alone," the women at the counter chimed. The man mumbled something in Spanish, then something in English. All I could understand was, "White people sending us poor people to war."

I paid the clerk, she gave me my milk, and I walked out the door. I was intent on not turning around but expected him to come after me.

It wasn't until one hour later that I heard the commotion.

I was sitting at my desk completing some paperwork when my phone rang. It was my secretary.

"Look, Monica," she said, "don't come out here. There's a crazy Hispanic man looking for you."

I could hear someone yelling in the background, "Where's that white woman? I saw her walk over here. Where is she?" My secretary placed her hand over the receiver, but I could still hear her say, "I don't know who you're talking about. Go home. You're drunk. Get some sleep."

"I won't leave until I see that white woman!" the man yelled. My secretary whispered through the phone that someone was looking for the security guard and then hung up.

I waited forty-five minutes before I called my secretary back.

"Is it safe to come out?" I queried.

"Yes," she said.

I walked to her office and was bombarded by taunts from my fellow employees.

"Hey, white woman!" they yelled. "What are you doing causing all this commotion?"

I shrugged my shoulders. When I reached my secretary's office, she told me the story of the Hispanic man with the yellow eyes. It appears that he was a Vietnam veteran who was suffering from post-traumatic stress disorder. He had been a normal twenty-year-old when he left the United States but came back suffering from hallucinations. He refused medication but coped by drinking. Every now and then, he would end up in the psychiatric hospital, would cope well for a while, but then stop his medication and start drinking again. He had no family. He blamed all white people for his problems and spent hours in the lobby talking to anyone who would listen. He was well-known in the community as being a very angry and unstable man.

"So how did you get him to leave?" I asked.

"We looked high and low for the security guard, but no one could find him. Mike finally calmed him down," she told me. Mike was one of the therapists.

The next day, I spoke to Mike and thanked him.

He said, "You know, I walked down the back hallway and out the back door to have a cigarette afterward, and I found the security guard hiding in the stairwell. He was literally shaking and worried that he would have to confront the man. I told him it had all been taken care of."

Poor guy, I thought, *first a German shepherd and now a psychotic, alcoholic Vietnam vet.*

For the next few weeks, I was vigilant every time I came to work, but I never saw the man with the yellow eyes again.

Domestic Violence

After my flight from Indiana, I landed in Ohio. I found a nice apartment complex to live in that was surrounded by woods. My apartment was on the ground floor, facing a ravine. A cemetery was located on the corner. *Nice and peaceful*, I thought.

My peace was to be shattered the third night after my move in.

I had spent the day unpacking, organizing, and cleaning. I wanted my apartment to be in order when I started my new job two days from then. I was exhausted, so went to bed early. A light sleeper, I needed to become accustomed to my new surroundings before I slept soundly. After several hours of tossing and turning, I finally fell asleep. I don't know how long I had been asleep when I was awakened by a loud thud. The sound was coming from the apartment above me. The thud was followed by a sound as if someone was dragging something very heavy across the floor. This was followed by the muffled sound of a woman's voice saying, "Stay away from me. Don't you come near me!" This was yet followed by the sound of breaking glass and again the sound of something heavy being dragged across the floor. I heard some grunts and imagined that a struggle was in process. I feared that the woman was being dragged across the floor.

Then, as suddenly as the commotion began, it ended. I lay in bed, frightened, worried, and anticipating more to follow. Silence. I didn't know what to do. Do I call the police? I waited some more. Nothing happened. I eventually fell back asleep.

The next evening, I was again awakened by noise above me. This time, the woman was plainly screaming for her pursuer to stay clear. I picked up the phone. The noise stopped. I waited, yet no further disruption. I was again frightened and worried. What was happening up there? Did I have an active imagination, or was a woman being pummeled? I decided to talk to the management the next day.

The next morning, I discovered that my neighbors above me were moving out. I passed them in the hallway as they were moving furniture to their van and tried to make eye contact with the woman. She avoided my gaze. Did I see a bruise around her eye?

New tenants moved in, who were quiet and kept to themselves. The peace in my apartment building, however, only remained for approximately two more months.

It was a night in early autumn, one of those nights where it is not hot, yet not cold—an in-between night where one could have been comfortable with or without open windows. I had my windows open. This time, I was not awakened by a loud thud, by arguing, or by any noisy commotion at all. This time, I was awakened by a woman moaning. The sound set my hair on end and cut me to the bone. She groaned as if she was in excruciating pain. "Someone . . . help me . . . please help me . . ."

I shot up straight in bed. There it was again—the moaning. "If someone can hear me . . . help me . . . please help me." This was not my imagination. I called the police and told them that I heard noises that appeared to be coming from the wooded ravine behind my apartment building. I told them that it sounded like a woman in great distress. I imagined her lying in the ravine, bleeding to death.

The police were at my door within minutes. By that time, the moaning had stopped. A policeman interviewed me and asked me again for details. I could see flashlights searching in the ravine below. I told the policeman that I was not certain where the woman was but that it had sounded as if it had come from the ravine. He told me that they had found nothing and thanked me for my information.

The next morning, I received a phone call from management. I explained what had happened. The manager thanked me for my report and assured me that the complex did not routinely rent to wife beaters. She told me that she had received complaints in the past about yelling from the couple on the top floor—the apartment that faced the ravine. She also told me, and for the life of me, I don't understand why, that a police officer lived in that apartment. I was stunned yet determined to help this woman who lived on the third floor.

As I left the building for the day, I taped the number of a domestic violence hotline near the mailboxes. When I came home in the evening, the number was gone.

That night, I had difficulty falling asleep. Suddenly, I thought I heard the woman moaning again. Was I mistaken? Someone slammed a window shut and turned on their air-conditioning unit. This I found odd as it was a cool evening. I strained my ears to listen for distress. I could hear nothing but the sound of the air-conditioning.

I wish they would turn that air off, I thought. *I can't hear anything.*

The next day, I put the hotline number up again. When I returned home, it was again gone. I did this for three days straight. On the fourth day, I did nothing. I didn't know if the number was getting into the hands of the woman, the perpetrator, or management. No one ever approached me about the number, so I just let it be. I didn't know what else to do. I didn't know who these people were, nor did I know if I wanted to become involved more than just anonymously.

The saga of the moaning woman appeared to be over with until I was approached by a neighbor several months later. Unbeknownst to me, my neighbor had also called the police regarding a disturbance. My neighbor informed me that the policeman was indeed beating up his wife and that he would turn on the air-conditioning unit in order to stifle his wife's screams. The policeman had been very angry that someone had reported the incidents.

No word on whether the woman received assistance, was sent to the hospital, or died—only word that management had asked them to leave.

If only she would have known about the cycle of violence, the use of tactics such as emotional abuse, sexual abuse, isolation, and intimidation to gain power and control. If only she would have known that these tactics would lead to physical abuse. If only she would have known about the honeymoon period after the physical abuse that is followed by more physical abuse. If only she would have known that she had the right to be treated with respect. If only she would have known that she had the right to preserve her dignity as long as she did not violate the rights of others.

If only.

The Blind Man

I came face-to-face with a gun one time. It was the summer of 2000, and I was a volunteer at a local public radio station. In appreciation of the work the volunteers did, the radio station gave a pizza party at a bowling alley. Bowling really wasn't my thing, but for some reason, I was right on that night. I really enjoyed throwing strikes and wondered when my luck would run out.

After two hours of bowling and socializing, I decided to call it a night. I turned in my shoes, said my goodbyes, and left the bowling alley. It was 9:00 p.m. on a Friday night in August in downtown Detroit. It was a warm seventy-eight degrees, and I grieved for the end of the long daylight hours. I had parked around the block, less than two minutes away, so thought nothing of walking to my car alone. I had grown up in Detroit during the turbulent '60s. Although crime was still an issue, Detroit seemed to be making a turnaround. I had never had any difficulties and always felt safe and secure.

I suddenly felt uneasy, however, when I saw the two men. I ignored their stare and crossed the street so I wouldn't have to walk in front of them. I clutched my purse close to me and held it tightly when I heard steps quickly approaching from behind. I increased my step and was only one car away from my own when the suspense overtook me. I looked over my shoulder to see a man with a baseball cap, thick-rimmed glasses, and shorts. His eyes had a cloudy gray film over them, as if he was blind, and they moved rapidly from side to side. He held a cup in his left hand and asked me for spare change. I shook my head and began to turn away when he raised his right hand to me ever so slightly. In it was a shiny revolver. My temper began to rise. How dare this man pretend to be in need! How dare he rob me!

I initially went for my change—he had asked for my change after all—but then was reminded that he had a gun, and it was pointing right at me. So I gave him some singles.

He raised the gun and yelled, "Give me a fifty. Give me a fifty!"

I was so angry; I yelled back at him, "I don't have a fifty."

He yelled again, "Give me a twenty!" I dug in my wallet and retrieved a twenty.

"That's all I have," I lied. He grunted and ran away.

I entered my car and just sat there. I had just been robbed . . . I had just been robbed . . . I had just been robbed by a blind man.

I didn't want to call 911 from my cell phone because I thought the men were still watching me. I had to drive right past them. I waited a few minutes and drove away. First, I drove to the radio station, hoping that someone would let me in so that I could call the police. They had a security system, but no one answered. I didn't know where the nearest police station was, and even if I did, I didn't feel safe leaving my car. I didn't feel safe remaining in Detroit, period.

So I drove to the police department in my hometown, a small suburb approximately thirty minutes from Detroit. Don't ask me how I made it there—I was in shock—one minute I was in Detroit, and the next, I was at the police station. The moment I walked through the doors of the station, I began to cry. I tried to maintain my composure as I walked to the intake desk but to no avail.

I sobbed. "I've just been robbed."

The police officer looked at me and asked, "Ma'am, how do you know that you've been robbed?"

Hmm, I thought. *Hmm . . . how do I know that I've been robbed? Wait a minute . . . don't tell me . . . I know the answer to this question . . . Hmm, how do I know that I've been robbed? This, I thought the most ridiculous question in the world! What do you mean, how do I know I've been robbed?*

I snapped back, "A man approached me, pointed a gun at me, and said, 'Give me your money.'"

"Oh," the policeman replied, "what kind of gun was it?"

I explained that I didn't know anything about guns, but that it was small enough to fit in his right hand, that it was silver, and that he had his index finger extended along the barrel. The policeman was not taking notes but continued his questioning.

Apparently, I answered the next question incorrectly because all hell broke loose.

"Where did this occur?" the officer asked.

"In Detroit," I answered.

The officer rolled his eyes and became very stern with me. "I can't help you! There's nothing that I can do for a crime that was committed in Detroit!"

I nodded my head and attempted to affirm that I was aware of this, but my sobbing was uncontrollable by this time. I was screaming in my head, *I just want a number that I can call to report the crime, that's all,* but the words wouldn't come out. I just sobbed while the police officer continued his tirade.

"What do you expect me to do for a crime that was committed in another city? You should have reported this in Detroit!"

I again nodded my head. Through sobs, I was finally able to begin explaining. "I know. But I didn't feel safe . . . they were watching . . . I couldn't call 911 . . . I didn't know where the nearest police station was . . . all I want is a number . . ."

"Lady, I don't have any numbers for you!" he responded. The officer then proceeded to educate me on the interplay between suburban police departments and that he could have easily helped me had the crime taken place in the suburbs. "This is not Detroit," the officer reminded me. "This is not Detroit," he said, shaking his head.

It suddenly became clear to me that this officer had no intention of being empathic, kind, or of helping me in any way. The phone rang at that time, and the officer answered it. I stood there in shock, retraumatized by a man in blue, the very person who was supposed to protect and defend. Wasn't it enough that I had just been robbed?

I tried to clear my mind and decided to go home and try my luck with a Detroit phone book. I turned around and began walking away. I got halfway to the door when the officer yelled at me, "Hey, lady! Wait!" He motioned for me to return to the desk. He was writing on a piece of paper as I approached the desk and hung up the phone. "Guess what," he said. "That was an off-duty Detroit police officer. He gave me this number for you to call. They can help you."

I didn't know if I should give the officer the finger or grab the number and run.

I took the piece of paper, thanked the officer, and drove home angry, shaking, and scared. When I arrived home, I called the number on the paper. A female police officer answered. She had the voice of an angel—in fact, I thought I heard a harp playing in the background—but then again, maybe it was just a siren. She took the information and informed me that a detective would be calling me in the morning. I thanked her for her kindness and hung up the phone.

I pulled out my wallet to see how much money I had left. I found a one-dollar bill.

The blind man left me with one dollar.

The blind man had left me with one dollar, and a feeling that I could never be safe in Detroit again.

My luck had just run out.

The Mumbler

It was a cold night in November when I met Joshua. I enjoyed dancing and had decided to sign up for a singles benefit dance for a local charity. The hall was located right on the Detroit River and had massive picture windows that highlighted the Windsor skyline. The hall was decorated with Christmas lights that glistened in the darkness. The stars twinkled, and the moon shone brightly as I gazed upon the river. I felt magic in the air and wondered if I would meet my true love that night.

I stood at the edge of the dance floor, listening to the music. Suddenly, I felt a light tapping on my shoulder. I turned around, and there he stood, strikingly handsome but somewhat sheepish in making his request to dance with me. I immediately accepted and was swept away by his nimble feet. We laughed, talked, and danced the night away as he carried me across the dance floor. At the end of the evening, we exchanged phone numbers and sealed the night with a kiss.

I was so excited when I got home, I could hardly sleep. In fact, I only found myself dozing when the phone rang at five in the morning. Who could that be? I picked up the phone but only heard mumbling at the other end.

"You'll have to speak more clearly, I can't understand you," I told the unknown caller.

"I've been lying in bed all night, just thinking about you," the man said.

My heart began to flutter. It was Josh! I sighed and stated, "Me too. In fact, I haven't been able to sleep that well at all."

He started mumbling again.

"You're mumbling again. You must really be tired. I can't understand you."

"Yeah," he said, "I've been working hard all day."

"You had to work today? I thought you said you had the day off," I replied.

After a moment of silence he said, "No, you must have misunderstood. I said I wished that I would have had it off, but I had to work."

"You have very demanding jobs. How do you do it? How do you cope with being a paramedic and a church deacon?" I asked.
There was another moment of silence and then mumbling again. Obviously, he wasn't coping well with it tonight!

"What's that?" I asked.

"I really want to hold you," he said.

"Yeah," I responded. "It was nice tonight, wasn't it?"

"I want to run my hands all over your body and . . . ," he stated.

I was taken aback by his straightforward approach.

"Don't you think you're moving a little too fast?" I asked. "I like to take things slowly."

He began to mumble again.

"What are you saying?" I was beginning to feel frustrated.

"What are you wearing?" he queried.

"You're really getting too personal. I don't even know you yet, and you're getting sexual. I want to get to know you first," I stated.

"What do you want to know about me?" he sighed.

"Well, tell me about your family. Do you have any brothers or sisters . . . are your parents still alive?"

"I have a younger brother and that's it. I'm named after my father, but he answers to Robert while I answer to Bobby," he explained.

"Wait a minute," I interrupted, "I thought you told me your name was Joshua!"

Another moment of silence, then, "Well, I legally changed my name to Joshua. It just made things easier. I don't get along that well with my good-for-nothing, alcoholic dad. I didn't want to be named after him."

Hmm. Sounded like Joshua really had some issues with his dad.

"So let's talk about something else," he grunted.

"OK. So what kind of car do you drive?" I asked.

"A 1999 Ford Escort," he replied.

"You're kidding me! Why didn't you say anything when you walked me to my car?" I, too, drove an Escort.

"What color are your panties?" he asked.

And this guy wanted to become a minister? I was becoming frustrated again.

"None of your business!" I replied.

"Are they purple?" he continued.

"I'm not telling you!" I responded.

"Come on, what color are they?" he pressed.

"Look," I said firmly, "if you continue talking like this, I'm hanging up the phone."

"Just tell me what color they are. Why won't you tell me?"

"I'm hanging up the phone now," I stated.

"Oh, come on!" he responded. "Why don't you tell me?"

I hung up the phone. Man, was he pushy!

The phone rang. I hesitated and then picked it up.

"Why won't you tell me?"

I slammed the phone down. Creep!

The phone rang again. I didn't pick it up. I lay in bed, fuming over the conversation. Ten minutes passed when the phone rang again. I didn't pick it up.

The rest of the day was uneventful as I tried to put the phone call out of my mind.

Monday rolled around, and I was getting ready for work. The phone rang. I hoped it wasn't my sister with bad news about my mother's health. My mom had never been the same after her double knee replacement surgery.

I picked up the phone.

"Why did you hang up on me?" he inquired angrily.

"Oh, it's you!" I responded. "Don't you get it? I'm not getting into any sex talk!"

"But why won't you tell me what color your panties are?" he pressed.

I hung up the phone, but he immediately called back. I didn't pick up the receiver. Who did he think he was? What a way to start out the day! I didn't have time for this nonsense!

That night, as I was sitting down to dinner, the phone rang. "I've got to get caller ID," I said to the dog. Although reluctant, I picked up the phone. It might be important.

"Hi, it's Josh," the voice said.

"Josh," I replied, "are you planning on talking nicely, or will I have to hang up on you again?"

"What are you talking about?" Josh asked.

"What do you mean?" I retorted. "You've been calling here, talking dirty, and I haven't appreciated it one bit!"

"What are you talking about?" he repeated.

"Oh come on," I said, frustrated, "you know what I'm talking about." I could feel my temperature start to rise.

"No, I don't," he said curtly, "I haven't spoken to you since the night we met!"

Silence.

I was stunned. Was he telling me the truth?

"You mean to tell me that you didn't call here yesterday at 5:00 a.m., or this morning at six forty-five?" I asked.

"I was asleep at five yesterday, and this morning I was performing CPR on a man having a heart attack at six forty-five," he explained.

"You're kidding me," I replied.

"No, I'm not kidding you!" Josh was angry. "Can you tell me what this is all about?"

"Let me get this straight," I responded. "You didn't call me yesterday, and you didn't call me this morning."

"No. I didn't call you until now. Frankly, this all sounds weird to me, and if you don't explain what you're accusing me of, I'll have to say goodbye!"

I told Josh about the phone calls but was still in minor disbelief. If Josh hadn't called, then who had?

"Didn't you recognize my voice?" Josh asked.

"No," I snapped. "Why would I? We just met!"

"Why would I tell you that my name was Bobby?" he responded.

I could feel my temperature reaching the boiling point.

"Because you didn't get along with your alcoholic father!" I said sternly.

"This is all too bizarre," Josh said. "Try to put yourself in my shoes. I don't know if I want to get involved with you. My last relationship ended because my girlfriend went bonkers over a pair of shoes that she claimed I owned . . . which I didn't . . . and now you're accusing me of making obscene phone calls! This is just all too weird!"

Reality was slowly sinking in.

I had been talking to an obscene phone caller! Not only that, I had actually tried to get to know the obscene phone caller. I had asked about his life; I had been attempting to have a relationship with an obscene phone caller!

I burst out laughing.

"I'm sorry, Josh," I said. "Do you see the humor in this? Neither of us knows if the other is telling the truth—not a good way to start a relationship, but funny nonetheless!"

Josh reluctantly agreed. We both tried to put the incident behind us. I talked to Josh for an hour on the phone and found out the truth about his family, his car, and his passions. I really liked this guy!

Two days later, the phone rang as I was getting ready for work.

"Have you calmed down now? What color are your panties?" he asked.

I hung up. Later that day, I called the police and talked to a detective about tracing my phone calls. Later that day, I also purchased caller ID.

As far as I know, Bobby never called back. It was months later when his name came up again. An acquaintance of mine who claimed to be psychic asked me, "Who's Bobby?"
"Bobby?" I asked.
"Bobby was an obscene phone caller that called me up a couple of months ago!"
"Well, regardless of who he is, you're about to hear some bad news about Bobby!" she responded. This just didn't make sense to me. How could I possibly hear bad news about a person whom I really didn't know, unless I really did know Bobby. Did I know Bobby?

Did I know Bobby?

Bobbi

I met Bobbi in aerobics class. She stood out like a sore thumb. Just a wisp of a woman, Bobbi was lethargic and acted as if she would rather be anywhere but aerobics class. She told me that signing up for aerobics had been a mistake, that she really had wanted Pilates; but the class was full, and she had no other recourse. I couldn't see her in a Pilates class either. Bobbi was not interested in any type of physical exertion, so signing up for any class at the gym was ridiculous.

Bobbi was living with her boyfriend, who I later discovered was secretly her husband. They had been together for several years and had decided to get married without the knowledge of their families. Not that their families would disapprove—just that the mental health pathology factor was so high on both sides they opted to avoid any drama at a formal wedding ceremony. Six months after I met Bobbi, she and her husband had a formal ceremony anyway, so the deception was for naught.

Bobbi and I met regularly for coffee after class. She would talk about how exhausting class was, and I would talk about how dissatisfied I was beginning to feel in my relationship with Josh. Bobbi gradually began revealing her dissatisfaction with her husband too. After I ended my relationship, our meetings seemed to focus on Bobbi's dissatisfaction with her marriage. I noted that Bobbi had never had anything good to say about her husband from day one. In the beginning, she joked about minor things such as toilet seat issues. But as time went on, Bobbi criticized his every move.

Then one day it happened. Bobbi stopped attending aerobics class. I called her at home, but she didn't return my calls. Two months later, I finally heard from her.

"You'll never guess what happened," she said. "My life has been hell . . . you'll never guess what happened." She was right. I couldn't guess, and nothing would have prepared me for what she told me next.

"My grandfather died," she said. "And I could kill my brother for what happened!"

Both of Bobbi's parents were deceased, killed in a car accident when Bobbi was still a child. Bobbi and her brother were raised by their grandfather.

"I'm so sorry. What happened?" I asked.

"My grandfather was in failing health. He was basically bedridden, but my brother chose to ignore that fact and decided to grant him one last wish. As my brother was his primary caretaker, he didn't discuss it with me and took him camping. Yes, camping!"

"Camping?" I asked in disbelief.

"Camping," she repeated. "My grandfather loved to camp, and my brother wanted a change of scenery. The stress of caring for my grandfather was just too much for him."

"How could your grandfather go camping if he was bedridden?" I queried.

"Good question," Bobbi replied. "He couldn't, but my brother ignored that fact and shoved him in the car anyway. I don't know how he was able to fit everything in his car, but he packed the gear, as well as my granddad, and off they went camping in the Upper Peninsula. Needless to say, it did not go well. My grandfather caught pneumonia and died before the excursion was finished. My brother, in a panic, rolled my grandfather up in a tarp and strapped him to the roof of the car . . ."

"What!" I yelled.

"Yes, he strapped him to the roof of the car. Do you know how windy it is crossing the Mackinac Bridge? Remember when that woman died when her car was blown off the bridge?" she asked.

"Yes, I remember. That happened several years ago. Wasn't she driving a Yugo?" I replied.

"I don't remember what she was driving, but my brother's car is small and that wind was whipping at my poor granddad's body attached to the roof. My brother had to stop and tighten the ropes—although he wasn't supposed to stop. It's a miracle my granddad didn't fly off that bridge," she said.

I couldn't believe what I was hearing. What compelled Bobbi's brother to take their grandfather camping in the first place?

Bobbi continued, "Well, they made it over the bridge safely, but then my brother had to stop to take a break. He decided to stop at a restaurant and get a bite to eat. So he stops in this town and pulls into the parking lot of a mom-and-pop restaurant. He parks the car, goes inside, and sits in a booth. After he eats, he leans his head back, exhausted, and falls asleep. Who knows how long he sleeps for . . . when he wakes up, he pays the bill and leaves the restaurant. The only thing is, the car is gone. Someone stole the car . . . with my granddad still attached to the roof!"

"Oh no!" I exclaim.

"Yes," she says, "someone stole my brother's car. Luckily, they found the car and the body at the other side of town. Apparently, the thief stopped to check his plunder, discovered what was in the tarp, and took off screaming. There were some witnesses at the scene and were able to give a description of the guy."

"Oh my gosh," I said. "I can't believe it. Did your grandfather . . . your grandfather's body . . . did they make it back home OK?"

"Yes. The police had to investigate, and after it was determined that no foul play had occurred, my brother rented a hearse to transport him home. The funeral home gave us a deal on it considering they had to drive it down here and then back again. I guess they felt sorry for my brother."

"And get this," she added, "my brother convinced my granddad to change his will right before he died so that he was the sole beneficiary."

"You're kidding . . . ," I said. I didn't know what else to say.

"Yeah, that son of a bitch," Bobbi said. "Now he's accusing me of taking money out of my granddad's account to use for my own selfish needs! I did take the money out of his account but at my granddad's request!" Bobbi continued to tell me that her granddad had been suspicious about her brother's intentions—little did he realize that he only intended on taking him camping—and had wanted Bobbi to take over his financial needs. She told me that she was having difficulty proving that she had the money legitimately and that she had planned on using it to cover funeral expenses. She had a court date in a few days.

I didn't hear from Bobbi again for another six months. She called me out of the blue and sounded worried. She told me that there was no progress in court as the hearings had been continued repeatedly. She also told me that the stress in her marriage was at its zenith and that she was filing for divorce. I invited Bobbi to a party I was hosting the following night—maybe it would help to get her mind off things.

Bobbi never showed up, and she never returned my phone calls—until six months later. She left a message on my voice mail stating that she had had enough of the stress, quit her job, left her husband, and moved to Vegas. Her plan was to become a showgirl. What better way to make use of her aerobics training?

I never heard from Bobbi again.

B Is for Baba

After nine good years of service, my laptop died. It was a slow, gradual death that afforded me the opportunity to remain in denial for two months; but after two months of experiencing squiggly lines, intermittent freezing, and spontaneous changing from lower—to uppercase letters, I decided it was time to lay my old friend to rest. The service tech at the computer store told me that I might be able to purchase a battery online; however, as the computer was so old, finding one might be an arduous task. The battery also might cost $250 or more. Adding that to diagnosis and repair costs, it would probably be best to buy a new computer. I leaned over the service counter, looked at the name embroidered on the tech's shirt, and said, "Thank you, A-1."

He laughed.

"Why are you laughing?" I asked.

"No one has ever called me that," he replied.

"Isn't that your name?" I asked.

"Oh no," he answered. "My name is Al."

Oh.

I went on my merry way and purchased a new laptop.

Now I'm the kind of person who many consider as living in the Stone Age. I don't have cable, and I don't have DSL. I have dial-up and have been very pleased with this service. After I purchased my laptop, I was eager to install my dial-up so that I could gain access to the Internet. I turned my laptop on for the first time and followed the easy-first-time-use instructions. I signed on and plugged the laptop in to juice up the battery. I waited until the battery was fully operational before I proceeded. Sure, icons were in different places, but it wouldn't take me long before I became accustomed to the computer. I put in my dial-up CD and followed the instructions—well, at least I thought I was following the instructions. For some reason, the computer wasn't recognizing the CD. After clicking on this and clicking on that, I decided to call for help. I hesitated briefly, debating whom to call: do I call the computer tech support, or do I call the dial-up tech support? I decided to call the computer tech guys.

A nice young man answered the phone. He had a Midwest accent like I, and for some reason, I imagined he was sitting in a cubicle in Colorado. I explained my problem, and this nice young man quickly set me straight. The phone call lasted approximately ten minutes; my dial-up was installed, and I was once again on my merry way.

Day two with my new computer arrived, and I found that the installation didn't take. This time, I decided to call the dial-up guys. This time, I knew exactly where I was calling—a small business in Ypsilanti, just a stone's throw from Ann Arbor. Again, the call went quickly, and the problem was easily resolved. The phone call lasted ten minutes.

Day three with my new computer arrived, and what a frustrating day it was! I turned my laptop on only to find that the juice was drained from the battery. Odd, I thought, but plugged the computer in. I waited until the battery was at 30 percent capacity before proceeding on. To my surprise, the dial-up connection that I had already installed twice was nowhere to be found. I decided to call that nice young man in Colorado again.

The phone rang, and I was placed on hold. After following several prompts, a man with a thick Indian accent answered. I explained my problem, and he asked me for my case number.

"Case number? Do you mean . . ." and I read off some numbers near the keyboard.

"No," he said, "what's your phone number?"

I gave him my phone number.

"It's not there," he replied. "What's the serial number?"

"Where do I find that?" I asked.

"On the bottom of the laptop," he said.

I turned the computer over but had some difficulty accomplishing this as it was still plugged in. I eventually found a box with several sets of numbers. I gave him the first set of numbers, which unfortunately, were not the serial number. I was beginning to get frustrated.

"No, ma'am. The other set," he said.

"Which set?" I responded. "There are two other sets."

I lucked out on my second try; however, this information was still not sufficient for the man with the thick Indian accent. I didn't know where to imagine he was sitting and did not want to assume that he was indeed in India.

So I pictured him sitting next to the nice young man in Colorado.

He asked me for my name and told me he had to create a "case" on me. I provided him with my name and address and again with my phone number and serial number.

"Now, how can I help you?" he asked.

I gasped. Hadn't he been listening? I took a deep breath and repeated my litany.

"So you're having problems with the dial-up and your battery. Is that right?" he asked.

"Yes," I responded.

"OK. Now here is what I want you to do . . . ," he stated. He instructed me to click on various icons, but the computer was moving as slow as molasses. I sighed loudly and informed him that the computer was not accepting the commands quickly.

"Yes, ma'am," he responded, "the dial-up is moving slowly."

"No," I said, "I'm not even connected to the dial-up yet. The computer is moving slowly."

"You have dial-up," the man said.

"Yes!" I snapped.

"Are you on the same line as the dial-up?" he asked.

I laughed and wanted to retort, "Do you think I'm that stupid?" Instead, I simply responded with a no. I thought a minute, and then I added, "I'm frustrated. The computer is moving very slowly. I'm sure you're just as frustrated with me."

The man asked me to inform him when the screen we were waiting for materialized. After a few minutes, the man asked me, "Is it there?"

"No," I answered.

A few minutes later, "Is it there?"

"No."

The man decided to ask me about the weather. I told him it was sunny and warm and asked him what the weather was like where he was.

"Also warm," he answered.

"And where are you?" I asked.

"What did you say?" he queried.

"Where are you? I'm in Detroit—where are you?"

"I'm in India," he said.

"India! Oh my gosh!" I stammered. I briefly got caught up in the fact that we were continents away. The man didn't seem to be impressed.

"What time is it there?" I asked.

"What day is it?" he asked me.

"What time is it? It's eleven in the morning here." I found myself speaking very slowly and loudly. He answered my question and then asked me if the violet light was on.

"The violet light?" I asked.

"Yes, the violet light," he responded.

"I don't have a violet light," I said.

"It should be on the front of the computer, next to the push in tab to open the laptop," he explained.

I looked but didn't see a violet light.

"I don't see a violet light," I said.

"Yes, the violet light. Find the violet light!" I could tell he was becoming more frustrated with our call.

"I see the battery light but no violet light. I'll look in the owner's manual and see if I can find it . . ."

I looked through the book but could not find a violet light. My eyes glanced up to the top of the keyboard and were stopped by a blue light. I looked in the owner's manual and discovered that this was the "wireless" light.

"Oh, the wireless light!" I exclaimed. "It's at the top of the keyboard."

Once we established that the wireless light was on, he was able to walk me through a set of instructions which simply meant insert the dial-up CD and follow the instructions! By this time, one hour had passed, and we hadn't even addressed the problem with the battery. The man suddenly announced that his supervisor was taking over. I guess he had had enough of me.

"Yes, ma'am. How can I help you?" the supervisor asked.

I took a deep breath and, in a very restrained voice, explained my problem. I asked if the battery could be the cause for the failure of the dial-up to remain installed. The supervisor did not answer my question but directed me through a series of windows. The supervisor's instructions were very confusing. I also had difficulty understanding his thick Indian accent, so I asked him to spell what command he was directing me to type. "*S* as in Sam, *N* as in Nicholas, and *B* as in BaBa," he said. *Baba?* I thought. *He must mean, like, Ali Baba.*

I repeated the letters to him, "*S* as in Sam, *N* as in Nicholas, and *B* as in Baba."

"Yes," he said. The computer would not recognize my command. I tried again. And again. And again.

It finally struck me that the supervisor was saying, "*P* as in papa." Once I discerned that, I was able to get to the window that he had been seeking. Unfortunately, the screen that he had been seeking had been the Total Health Care screen—a screen that I had already accessed. The information on this screen simply stated that the battery was in good condition.

By this time, two hours had passed. I was beyond being frustrated—I was very close to being homicidal! I calmed myself down and asked the supervisor what the longevity of the battery was.

"Yes, ma'am. It depends on how often you use your computer. Some batteries last several years . . ."

I interrupted him, "No. I mean on a day-to-day basis."

"Yes, ma'am," he responded, "as I was saying, it depends on how often you use your laptop per day. Some batteries last several years . . ."

I had had enough by then, thanked him, and was resigned to the fact that my battery would probably only have a daily life span of a few hours.

Two months have passed now, and I've become more acquainted with my new computer. Unfortunately, two days ago, my trial antivirus subscription ran out. When I had purchased my laptop, I also purchased an antivirus CD, not realizing that the computer came with the subscription. So instead of sending the CD back to the manufacturer, I decided to install it. I've installed antivirus software before, which has been relatively easy. This time, however, would not be the case. I started at 9:00 a.m. and by 8:00 p.m. was still not successful. I finally packed up my computer and headed to the computer store.

Unfortunately, A-1 was nowhere in sight.

I explained my problem to the tech who appeared to be listening intently. He nodded, rolled his eyes, and laughed when I told him that I had been working on the installation for eleven hours. This I took in good humor as I was presenting it with humor. The tech turned my computer on, scrolled through various windows, then stated, "The antivirus is nowhere to be found."

I nodded.

He stared at me.

"Well," he stated, "you could take it home and try again, or you could leave it here and we could install it."

Hadn't he been listening?

"I've washed my hands clean of this computer—it's in your hands now," I responded.

Yesterday evening, I was able to pick my laptop up. So far, I have had no problems with it: the antivirus appears to be installed, I've saved my cell phone minutes for another day, and I'm thinking about purchasing some stock in Valium for the next time that I have to cope with tech support.

The Sure Thing

I was listening to a local radio station the other day, which was having a contest about sure things. They asked for people to e-mail them about a sure thing that had gone bad in their lives. This led me to reflect on my own life and of all the sure things that had somehow gone wrong.

The year 1998 was the perfect example—everything went wrong, from beginning to end. That was the year that I turned forty, my boyfriend and I broke up, my dog came down with encephalitis, and my identity was stolen. Turning forty wasn't a particularly traumatic event for me, except that my boyfriend and I were having difficulties, and I just didn't feel like celebrating. I had decided a few months previously to take a break at a small health spa in Iowa. At the time, my boyfriend had decided to go too, but as the time came nearer, he changed his mind. So off I was by myself to the health spa in Iowa.

I was not concerned that I was traveling by myself. I had done this numerous times, both in the States and abroad. I loved to travel, and flying was second nature to me. Well, flying on jumbo jets, not commuter planes, that is! My itinerary was to land in a small town in Illinois and grab a connection to another small town in Iowa where I would be picked up by the spa shuttle and be driven for another 1½ hours to my destination. I had an appointment with the spa doctor midmorning, but I should have no difficulty making this appointment.

My problems started when I landed in Illinois.

I found my departing gate easily. I had thirty minutes to kill, so I decided to read a magazine. I had brought the book *Don't Sweat the Small Stuff*...

109

and it's all small stuff but wasn't in the mood to crack it open. The wait went by quickly, and soon we began boarding. I was surprised to see the other passengers scramble to stand in-line. Why were they in such a hurry to board? I snickered at their foolishness as I stood in the back of the line, the very last passenger. I shook my head in disbelief as the passengers ran to the plane as they passed through the gate. A steward stood at the head of the line, holding the rope he had just removed that separated the waiting area from the boarding area. He was counting as the passengers passed in front of him. I could hear him as I approached, "fifteen, sixteen, seventeen," *Boom!* That was it! He placed his arm in front of me and hooked the rope back up to the stand. No more passengers allowed! I looked behind me. There was no one there. What is this!

"I'm sorry, m'am, but you can't board," he said.

"Why not?" I asked.

"Because you're the eighteenth passenger," was his response.

"And so?" I asked again.

"The plane can only hold seventeen passengers plus luggage. You would make the plane too heavy. I'm sorry, but you can't board," he stated.

"No, you don't understand—I have a doctor's appointment in Iowa . . . ," I attempted to explain.
The steward would have nothing of me. He turned around and walked away.

I approached the airline desk, furious. The woman behind the desk braced herself for my attack.

"I don't understand why I'm not being allowed on board," I started peacefully.

"The plane is already full," the woman responded.

"But there are only seventeen passengers on board," I stated.

"And you're number eighteen, which would put the plane over its limit. I can give you a voucher . . . ," she said.

"I don't want a voucher!" I cut her off and was beginning to really get angry. "You don't understand! I have a doctor appointment at eleven. I have to be on that plane!"

"I'm sorry, m'am. The best I can do is to offer you a voucher for a round-trip ticket anywhere in the continental United States good for one year," she said.

"Let me explain," I said. "I am flying from Michigan to Iowa specifically for this doctor appointment. I have to be on that plane!"

"I'm sorry, ma'am . . . ," she attempted to respond.

"I have to be on that plane! Can't you see if another passenger would switch with me? I'm certain that someone would be willing to do that, once they know my situation," I said.

"I'm sorry, m'am, but the plane is already on the runway. Here's your voucher," she stated.

"Already on the runway?! But I have to be on that plane!" I said sternly.

The woman turned from me and began helping the next customer. I didn't budge.

"When is the next plane to Iowa?" I asked.

"In six hours," she responded.

"Six hours!" I was furious. They never mentioned that this might happen to me when I booked the flight. What kind of Podunk operation was this?

"You might as well make yourself comfortable," a man said from behind me. "That's what happens with commuter planes. You got to be the first in-line."

"I can't believe this is happening!" I said to him. "I'll miss my appointment! Do you have any idea how much money I paid to get that appointment?" I gathered my belongings and walked over to a bench. I called the spa and explained the situation. They were friendly and understanding, cancelled the appointment, and told me that the shuttle would be waiting for me in Davenport. All I could think about was the money I had flushed down the toilet. I was missing the entire day—not only for meeting with the doctor, but also for my massage, vegetarian lunch, and yoga class! How could this be happening?

I looked through my carry-on and found my *Don't Sweat the Small Stuff . . . and it's all small stuff* book. "I'm sorry, but this is not 'small stuff,'" I fumed to no one in particular.

I opened the book and began to read. The words weren't registering, however, as I repeatedly found myself spewing expletives over the situation. Suddenly, the words took hold, and I questioned the relevance of the incident considering the big scheme of things. I looked at the voucher and thought, *I suppose it won't matter. I always wanted to go to San Francisco.* I began to calm down and accept the fact that I would be there for six more hours—and you'd better believe that I'd be the first in-line!

The wait was long and boring. I finished the book quickly and wandered around the airport for a good portion of the time. I made certain that I was first in-line for boarding and was shocked to discover how small the aircraft was. No wonder they only allowed seventeen passengers on board. Since I had never been on a commuter plane before, I didn't know what to expect. I buckled my seat belt and waited for departure. The trip down the runway was loud and bumpy. The ascent was no different, nor was the entire flight to Davenport. I had never been on such a rough flight before. I wondered if I would be suffering from whiplash by the time we landed. Luckily, the flight went quickly.

I found myself in a small lobby barely bigger than my own living room when I disembarked. I looked around the room and saw people standing in the ticket line, people looking at maps, and people greeting each other. I saw an obese man standing at the doorway. He wore dirty bib overalls and a sleeveless blue shirt. His arms were covered in motor oil. He donned an old baseball cap that covered greasy dark hair. His toothless grin blocked the sparkle in his blue eyes. Don't ask me how, but I knew immediately that I had made contact with my driver as soon as our eyes met.

"Are you the one going to the health spa?" he asked me. I nodded. "My wife is in the car. I hope you don't mind. She came along for the ride," he explained. He didn't offer to take my luggage, just turned around and walked out the door. I followed him sheepishly, thinking that my trip from hell was not quite over. He approached a rusty old Chevy and opened the trunk. "You can put your bags in here," he said. I stared inside the trunk. It contained a toolbox, several opened cans of motor oil, and a ripped bag of kitty litter. I shook my head and told the man that I would take my bags with me in the backseat. "I want to check my hair dryer. I think it was crushed during the flight," I lied. I entered the backseat and fiddled with my bags. It wasn't until the man started the car that I remembered his wife was "along for the ride." I looked up to find a rotund woman with ruddy cheeks smiling at me. She was not toothless. She did smell of alcohol, however. She attempted to shake my hand but changed her mind midstream. It was awkward trying to reach over the backseat.

"Oh, what the hell," she said, waving her hand to me instead. "Hi, my name is Alice, and this here is Julius. We hope you enjoy your ride to the spa!"

I introduced myself and thanked the couple for their hospitality.

And so we were off!

The ride was uneventful, if you consider 1½ hours of knock-knock jokes uneventful. Periodically, Julius would swerve, Alice would scream, and Julius would accuse Alice of being drunk and overreacting. I tried ignoring the two, yet being pleasant when spoken to, I also tried remembering what I had read in the book. And if this was the shape the shuttle was in, what did the spa look like? My boyfriend was the one who had recommended it—just wait until I spoke to him again—I'd give him a piece of my mind! But I didn't have to reprimand him. The spa was beautiful and everything I had hoped it would be. I met with the doctor, received my massages, took my yoga classes, and toured the grounds. It was very relaxing. It turns out that the shuttle had broken down on its way to pick me up, so the driver called his cousin's brother-in-law, who was a mechanic, to help him out. They couldn't fix the problem, so his cousin's brother-in-law picked me up while the driver waited for a tow truck. Julius was not the shuttle driver, nor was he driving the shuttle—he was just the cousin's brother-in-law. My return trip to the airport was in a newly repaired van, complete with air-conditioning and a very articulate driver.

All right. So you think that's the end of the story? Almost.

I landed back in Michigan, relaxed and in one piece after the weekend at the spa. I waited at the gate for my boyfriend, but he never showed. I went to baggage claim after waiting fifteen minutes, found my baggage, then waited some more. He finally came running up to me, out of breath, apologizing profusely. He had had car problems but eventually got the problem fixed. When we arrived home, I noticed some tape stuck to the front door.

"What's this?' I asked.

"Oh, remember when I left you that note before you left?" he responded. I looked puzzled and shook my head but didn't pursue it. I knew he was lying, but I wasn't planning on sweating the small stuff.

He moved out within the week. It turns out that he was involved with another woman, although he was living with me, and had spent the weekend in Toledo with her.

So much for a sure thing.

The moral of the story is, of course, not to become anxious over the challenges in your life. As a result of the airport fiasco, I was able to spend my birthday the next year in California. I also was able to release myself from an unhappy relationship and move on.

See, it really didn't matter in the big scheme of things.

Etiquette

Michigan is in a bad economic state. The budget is in the hole, people are being laid off, benefits are being cut, and houses are in foreclosure. The legislature recently shut down for a few hours because they couldn't agree on how to solve the budget problem. What they finally decided to do was to raise the income tax to 4.35 percent and to raise the service tax to 6 percent. This means that such services as baby shoe bronzing, balloon-o-grams, palm reading, astrology services, and phrenology services will see an increase in their service tax. You may ask, "What exactly are phrenology services?" I, too, was curious along with everyone else in Michigan, so I looked it up in the *Webster's Seventh New Collegiate Dictionary*. This dictionary was presented to me by the local newspaper when I won my grade spelling bee in elementary school. The newspaper had my name engraved on the cover. It's misspelled.

Regardless of the spelling and regardless of the age of the dictionary, here is what I found: "phrenology, n: the study of the conformation of the skull as indicative of mental faculties and character." Now that you mention it, I do remember hearing something about this as an undergrad, that there was a science of studying the bumps on a person's head that determined a person's mental condition. Hmm. And just how many people practice phrenology in Michigan? According to a local news station, none. That's right, zero. What were the Michigan lawmakers thinking? Maybe they had too many bumps on their heads to realize that this would not create any revenue.

I am grateful that I at least have a job. Our contract is up, however, and rumor has it that we will not receive a raise this year. Tough news to swallow when the income tax is increasing. Prices are already high. People are worried about how they will be able to pay for such routine things as gasoline and groceries. How will we be able to survive when our paychecks are shrinking?

I stopped purchasing produce at the grocery store a long time ago. Grocery-store produce was just too expensive and was not of high quality. Instead, I shop at the farmers' market—the prices are fair, and the quality is good. The one thing I hate about the farmers' market, however, is the patrons. It starts in the parking lot. If you don't time it correctly, you will hit a traffic jam. There are no arrows painted on the cement to direct the flow of traffic, so people drive in all directions. Also, people drive very fast through the parking lot, hoping to gain access to the prime parking spaces. Sometimes the opposite is also true—people drive so slowly because they are in fear of (a) being run down by another automobile or (b) missing a prime parking space.

I've been behind cars that suddenly stop for no apparent reason. I've also been behind cars that have their right-turn signal on but turn left into a parking spot. Drivers also seem to believe that they have the right of way instead of pedestrians. It has happened to me on numerous occasions that I have almost been run over by a car that is backing out of a parking space. It's also happened to me that the person parked next to me left their shopping cart behind my car as I was trying to back out of my space.

I was forced to go to the farmers' market today because I ran out of produce. I tried to time it so that I missed the crowds, but unfortunately, I arrived there fifteen minutes too early. During the week, it's best to arrive after 7:00 p.m. On the weekends, it's best to arrive after 4:00 p.m. I arrived at 3:45 p.m. I knew I was in trouble but reminded myself to take my time and just flow with whatever happened.

I followed a Mercedes into the parking lot. The driver hesitated slightly, put his right-turn indicator on, and turned left. I unfortunately followed to the left where there appeared to be more available parking spaces. The Mercedes proceeded ahead for a brief period and then quickly turned right down an adjacent lane. I proceeded straight ahead and found a parking space near the back of the lot. I parked my car and looked for a shopping cart. If I walked down the adjacent aisle, I could pick up a cart that had been abandoned in the middle of a parking space. As I approached the cart, a car was approaching me. It was the Mercedes. The car slowed down. Just as I placed my hands on the cart, the Mercedes began to honk his horn. *Is he honking at me?* I wondered. I pushed the cart out of the parking space and smiled at the driver. He waved his hands frantically in the air, showing me that he was upset with me. I surmised that he believed I had left the cart there in an attempt to prevent him from parking. I smiled again, nodded, and said to him, "There you go, the space is all yours." He gave me the finger.

Once inside the market, I parked my cart and walked through the store, gathering the items that I needed. I have learned from experience that the market is no different from the parking lot: congested, confusing flow of traffic, and little or no regard for others. Sometimes it is best to park your shopping cart in order to avoid unexpected traffic jams and cranky customers. The important thing to remember is to place an item in your cart before you abandon it; otherwise, someone will abscond with it. I remembered to place a loaf of bread in mine before I cruised through the rest of the store. Other than the usual dancing for position through the aisles (even without a cart), I had little difficulty collecting my items. I was surprised to find the checkout lines were short. I entered a line that had one person in it. As I waited my turn, I glanced at the line next to me. There, I saw a little girl of about five years old with curly black hair and big pink sunglasses. She held an apple in one hand and picked her nose with the other. I laughed and turned my attention to the line on my opposite side. There stood a man of about thirty-five, picking the wax out of his ear with his car key. I watched him stick the key in his ear, turn it around, pull it back out, and remove the wax from the end. I was reminded of an incident that I observed when I last visited a local museum. As I was standing in-line in the women's room, I heard a woman in one of the stalls talking. As she stood up, I could see under the door that she flushed the toilet with one of her feet. When the door opened, it was revealed that she was talking on her cell phone. The woman apparently thought nothing of this, but the rest of us in-line looked at one another with distain. I almost said something to the woman but then thought otherwise.

With the nose picker to my right and the ear picker to my left, I decided it was best to turn my attention to my own checkout line. I checked out without incident.

I was surprised to see that the parking lot had emptied so quickly. There were few cars left, and I was able to pull out of my spot easily. I drove to the end of the aisle and stopped. A Toyota was slowly driving down the aisle perpendicular to me. "No," I said to myself. "No, don't you dare!"

Sure enough, he stopped right in front of me. I was blocked in. I glared at the driver. He smiled at me and waved.

As I sat there, waiting for the car to move, I pondered, "Do I put my finger in my nose, in my ear or give him the finger while I wait?"

I decided to wave back at him, and when I was able to turn right, I muttered under my breath, "Where's a phrenologist when you need them?"

The Yoga Class

I was becoming overly stressed at work, irritable, cranky, and generally miserable. I couldn't sleep at night and replayed the activities and interactions that had occurred during the day. It was at that time that I decided to take yoga. Yoga would certainly improve my mood, my sleep, and my concentration. So I joined a class at the local Y and entered the class with high expectations.

I arrived fifteen minutes early on the first night of class, complete with latex pants, cotton tee shirt, and meditation mat. Four other women had already staked their claim to a piece of the floor and were talking to a bubbly blonde woman in the front of the room. This woman had her hair up in a ponytail, which swayed to and fro when she spoke. She came from Texas and spoke with a drawl. Her body was trim. She wore latex pants and a sports bra, accentuating her muscular upper body. She was twenty-eight years old, and she was our teacher.

Incense filled the room, and I could feel my head begin to throb. For some reason, incense and I do not relate well—I usually develop a headache and become nauseous when around this burning menace.

This night was no different.

I scoped the room for a spot as far away from the incense as possible. I chose a spot in the back of the room, isolated from the others. As the night progressed, however, the room filled up, and I was no longer isolated. A total of twenty people had reported for this evening's class. Most of the students were women, but two men participated as well. The ages ranged from the teens to sixty. The only reason I knew this was because the sixty-year-old made certain everyone in the room knew her age. She was an interesting-looking woman, slightly over five feet tall, chubby, and with pitch-black hair. She had one streak of gray that went from her forehead to her shoulders. She spoke with a thick Spanish accent. She told me that her name was Juanita and that she had arrived from Spain five years ago. Her husband had died, and she moved to the Midwest to be with her children. She spoke fondly of her days in Spain, of her husband, and of her children; then she pulled out her pictures. I had expected the pictures to be of her family, or even of her favorite places in Spain, but all the pictures were of clouds. "This one," she said, "is the spaceship that abducted me and took me to planet Zircon. They're a friendly race, the Zirconians. Had they asked me to go with them, I would have gladly gone willingly!" I looked at the picture and nodded. The picture was of clouds . . . clouds! I didn't see a spaceship in sight, not that I know what a spaceship looks like, but these pictures were of ordinary, puffy, run-of-the-mill cumulus clouds. I stared at the pictures and hesitated before asking, "Where are the spaceships?"

She laughed at me and pointed at the clouds. "Well, they're right there!" she said. I didn't know if I should admit that I didn't see the spaceships or if I should pretend that I did. She must have sensed my hesitancy as she added, "If you take a pair of binoculars and put 26 mm film over the end of them, then look at the sun with them, you'll see your Presbyterian hymnal." Don't ask me what this statement had to do with anything—if I thought I was at a loss for words before, I was really at a loss now. Luckily, we were interrupted by the group of women giggling with the instructor.

"Oh, Marla, you have the cutest accent," one of them said.

"Why thank y'all," our instructor replied. Thankfully, Juanita left to investigate the commotion in the front of the room. I remained standing next to my meditation mat, scrutinizing the room, wondering how all these students happened to sign up for the course. I especially wondered about the men—they both appeared to be in their forties; one was skinny, balding, and had a bad comb-over; and the other had a paunch and strode like a cowboy who was saddle sore. I wondered if they knew that the instructor was a bubbling twenty-eight-year-old blonde and if they were going through a midlife crisis. The men chose to sit in the back, near me. Juanita chose to sit in the row ahead of us. The teenagers sat in the front row, along with the giggling women.

It was time to begin, and Marla announced that she unfortunately had to cut the class short by thirty minutes, but the time would be made up at a later date. This meant that we only had fifteen minutes to complete the yoga stretches and fifteen minutes to meditate. I didn't like the way this class was beginning.

Everyone sat down as Marla began to demonstrate the stretches.

"Of course, I make this look so easy," she bubbled, ponytail swaying as she spoke. She started us out lying on the floor and directing us to grab our knees. We were then to rock gently from side to side. Through the moans and groans of the people around me, I actually began to feel my back loosening up. She then had us position our bodies in the "wheelbarrow" stretch, followed by the "candlestick."

The "candlestick" is my personal favorite; you lie on the floor and bring your legs straight above you. Don't ask me why this pose is so relaxing, but I find myself closing my eyes and nodding off to sleep. Over time, this became troublesome for me; as the rest of the class would move on to the next pose, I was deep in trance. When I asked Marla how to remain awake during this pose, she simply stated, "Keep your eyes open."

Oh.

But on this first night of the "candlestick," I didn't fall asleep. How could I? Between the waves of nausea from the incense came another pungent smell. The source of the smell was a mystery at first, a silent bomb that quickly became a short explosive outburst. Yes, the man sitting next to me had a horrible case of flatulence. No wonder he sat in the back. I was just hoping that the rest of the class didn't think it was me.

The meditation came next. Marla instructed us to sit in a comfortable position with our eyes closed. She then explained that we were to take a deep breath in, hold it, and slowly exhale. We were to repeat this three times. She continued to explain that this was to be followed by chanting *who* very slowly for five minutes. This would be followed by silently meditating on whatever crossed our minds.

"OK. Ready?" Marla asked. "Take a deep breath in . . . hold it . . ."

I had silently counted to ten when she instructed us to release our breath.

"Take another deep breath . . . hold it . . ." I counted to myself again and began to relax deeply.

"One more time . . . ," Marla stated. "Hold it . . . now relax." There was a moment of silence before Marla was to begin chanting . . . what were we supposed to chant again?

My thought was interrupted by Juanita bellowing, "Jewww."

"Jew?" I asked myself. Did I really hear her say *Jew*?

"Jewww," Juanita chanted again.

Juanita had jumped the gun and started chanting before Marla did, and apparently, she was confusing her Spanish with her English.

"Jewww," Juanita chanted once more.

I peered through my closed eyes to find a very flabbergasted Marla attempting to speak. Every time she opened her mouth, Juanita jumped in and chanted, "Jewww." Finally, Marla gathered her composure and interjected, "Whooo."

Juanita didn't budge. "Jewww," she chanted back.

Marla became louder, "Whooo," she replied.

Juanita took this to mean that she too should chant louder. "Jewww," she bellowed.

Marla became louder yet, "Whooo."

Juanita responded in kind. It was dueling banjos. The rest of the class tried to help Marla out by chanting with her, but Juanita was not taking the hint. In fact, she tried to bring the group into one cohesive unit and yelled, "All together now! Jewww!"

No one joined in; however, suddenly I felt something brush against my leg. I opened my eyes to see the flatulent man crawling on all fours across my meditation mat. He was headed in Juanita's direction. I wondered what he was up to, and I was soon to find out. When he reached Juanita's mat, he tapped her on the shoulder and said very sternly, "Shut up!"

He then crawled back to his mat and began chanting again as if nothing had happened. Juanita appeared to be taken aback but stopped her loud chanting. Marla, having reached her threshold of frustration yelled, "It's *who*, not *Jew* y'all!"

There was silence in the room.

Marla seized the opportunity and began to very quietly chant, "Whooo." For five minutes, we chanted, and then we reflected silently.

I reflected on whether or not the space aliens were coming after Juanita. I hoped they weren't coming after me.

Ghost Story

It had been a very busy and exciting day. A friend of mine asked if I would be interested in attending a Tigers game. I was thrilled to go and was looking forward to seeing my first game in the new stadium. We had wonderful seats near the Tiger dugout. Unfortunately, no shade was to be found, but that didn't matter—the game was riveting, and the energy in the stadium was high. I have to admit I felt only slightly guilty watching the game at Comerica Park. Loyal to Tiger Stadium, I felt pangs in my heart, knowing that the old gem was scheduled for demolition. The new park was beautiful though, and I could watch the game without obstruction. The game was sold out, the crowd glued to the action on the field—a nail-biter—the Tigers lost in the eleventh inning.

I was exhausted when I arrived home. I slumped in the sofa and looked out the window in my sunroom. Too tired to turn the television set on, I sat in the quiet for several minutes. My eyes fell upon the stack of books, awaiting my summer reading enjoyment. I recalled a book I had glanced through at the bookstore that addressed the topic of paranormal activities. It provided several examples of these types of incidents, including those of spirits who had not realized that they were deceased yet. These misfortunate souls would go about their daily activities and become frustrated when they could not perform simple tasks such as drinking a cup of coffee or turning a doorknob. *Interesting*, I thought, *but how does that work? How does one lose their way to heaven, and how does one not realize that they are deceased?*

I was too exhausted to ponder the issue further, so I decided to go to sleep.

I slept soundly until 4:20 a.m. when I was suddenly aroused by the sound of beeping. The noise was loud and appeared to be coming from the foot of my bed. I had recently purchased an air purifier and had it placed on a table next to the wall near the foot of my bed. The noise sounded as if the purifier was malfunctioning and was changing its own settings. Although I did not have my glasses on, I could clearly see that the noise was not emitting from the purifier—the lights were not flashing, and the settings were not changing. I laid my head back down and sighed. The noise continued. I debated on whether or not to investigate. I had left my bedroom door open and could see into the hallway. Suddenly, a white light appeared at the end of the hallway where the kitchen and the living room intersected. *Probably just the paperboy delivering the newspaper*, I thought. I continued to look down the hallway when the light disappeared. It was replaced by a flashing light, the kind that you see when you are in a room and someone is watching television in the dark in another room.

Is someone watching television in my sunroom? I wondered. I squinted hard and stared intently. The flashing did not stop. My heart began to race. *Oh my god! Someone is in my house and watching television!* I thought.

I tried to calm down and think clearly. I wanted to remain in my bed and crawl under my covers, but my better judgment told me not to.

"What if someone was really in the house by mistake, watching TV . . . and eating popcorn?" I asked myself. I remembered a friend telling me that she once got up in the middle of the night to find a man sleeping on the floor in her living room. He had attended a party down the street, had been drunk, and somehow was able to enter her house unnoticed until the wee hours of the morning. I imagined a similar incident unfolding before my very eyes. My mind quickly scanned all the horror movies that I have seen—a person leaves the protection of one room to investigate some sinister noise in another location in the house. As this person is walking down the hallway, the audience yells, "No, don't go there!" Of course, the person cannot hear the audience and comes face-to-face with some horrific monster.

I reached for my glasses on the nightstand. Ever since my cat had accidentally knocked my glasses off the nightstand and broke them, I kept them inside my eyeglass case. This particular case was sealed with Velcro. I attempted to open the case slowly so as not to make a sound. The Velcro was holding tight; I had to open it quickly. "Rip," the eyeglass case shouted.

Oh great, I thought, *the intruder heard that one!* I held my breath and waited.

No footsteps.

It suddenly occurred to me that I could see into the sunroom from my bedroom window. My house was L shaped, so I could peer into the sunroom undetected if I moved slowly. The sofa was facing away from the bedroom, so if someone was sitting on it, I would not be noticed. Also, since my cats had a habit of crawling through the slats of the blinds, I routinely left the blinds positioned so that the cats could easily sit under them without disturbing them. Since the blinds did not run from ceiling to sill, I could see into the sunroom and determine if the television set was indeed on.

My heart raced as I crept out of bed. I took a deep breath and peered around the bedroom curtains. The sunroom was completely dark—the television set was not on. So what was making that beeping noise, and what was flashing?

The microwave?! Was someone using the microwave in the kitchen?

I glanced around the room. Unfortunately, my portable phones were in the living room and kitchen. My landline phone was in the bedroom—it would do me no good when I left the room to investigate, and at this point, I didn't have enough evidence to call the police. I looked around the room for a weapon. My baseball bat was in the basement. A pair of scissors was perched on my dresser, but they weren't long enough—I wanted some distance between me and the intruder. I also didn't want to actually harm anyone, especially myself should the scissors be used against me. The only thing I could think to use was the laundry basket that was sitting near the air purifier. I could use the basket as a barrier between me and my unwanted guest. Although flimsy, I could also possibly swing it in the direction of the intruder thereby fending him off, or throw the basket over his head.

I turned the basket over and emptied my clean clothes onto the floor. I took one last deep breath and entered the hallway, turning on all the lights as I strode to the kitchen. Once there, I could clearly see the time flashing on the microwave. It was set for thirty-three minutes and thirty-three seconds and instructed an unknown person to "press Start. High." I quickly glanced around the room. Not a soul was present except for three of my cats. I allowed the microwave to continue flashing while I investigated the rest of the house. I was the only occupant besides my cats . . . but only three cats had been accounted for.

At 4:20 a.m., your mind thinks of the worst—someone must have placed my fourth cat inside the microwave.

I placed my hand on the microwave door, hesitated, and threw the door open. The microwave was empty.

"Boy, that's a relief," I said aloud. I shut the door and cleared the time. The microwave immediately reset itself to thirty-three minutes and thirty-three seconds. I stared at the microwave momentarily before I attempted to clear it again. As soon as I reached for the clear button, the machine beeped louder and flashed more rapidly. I pressed the button, but the machine would not clear. I pressed again. It still would not clear. It did not accept my command until the third attempt. I stood there, amazed. Don't ask me why, but these two thoughts came into my head: it's a good thing that I don't have to use the restroom, and Jesus was thirty-three years old.

I stood in front of the microwave, waiting for it to set its own time again. Nothing happened.

I spoke to the microwave, "I know you want me to press the start button, but I'm not falling for it! What if you explode?!" I said. Suddenly, I remembered the chapter in the paranormal book. What if there was a ghost in my house, and what if it didn't realize that it was dead, and what if it was hungry and was trying to microwave popcorn in my oven? I pondered this a moment and then said aloud, "OK. I'll compromise with you. I'll set the timer for three minutes." I set the timer, pressed start, and waited. Nothing unusual happened, and at the end of the time, the oven shut itself off.

"Are you happy now?" I snapped.

I left the kitchen in a huff, laundry basket in hand, complaining that I had been awakened at 4:20 a.m. for a stupid microwave. When I entered my bedroom, I looked at the ceiling and stated very loudly, "If you are trying to tell me something, I'm not getting it! Waking me up at 4:20 in the morning only scares me. If you want something, save it for daylight!" I then crawled into my bed and slept fitfully for two more hours.

At 6:30 a.m., I was awakened by a beeping noise in the kitchen. The microwave was setting itself again. I guess it took my request literally. By that time, the sun had risen. I got up to cancel the time, and the oven immediately reset itself. This went on periodically for the next four hours.

Two days have gone by now, and the microwave ghost has not reappeared. I hope it found its destination. As for me, I've retrieved my old baseball bat from the basement and have placed it strategically in my bedroom. I've also changed the location of my portable phones, have finally put away my clean clothes that I dumped on the floor, and have returned to feeling guilty about attending Comerica Park.

Ponderings

A person has a lot of time to think as they are training for and/or completing a marathon. Here are some issues that I've pondered during the course of my marathoning.

If anyone has the answers to these questions, please let me know what they are—I am eager to cross these items off my list of ponderings and begin a new list of issues to obsess about.

- ❖ Why is it that pebbles become lodged between my sock and the inside of my shoe when I power walk—I mean, how is this even possible? How is it possible that something so tiny can enter my shoe as I'm walking? Why does this only happen when I power walk and not when I run? And why does the pebble feel like a boulder inside my shoe?
- ❖ Is it worth it to stop and empty my shoe? What are the chances that the pebble will work itself back out? Conversely, what are the odds that a pebble will enter my shoe to begin with?
- ❖ Why are professional basketball players allowed to chew gum on court? Do they ever accidentally swallow or choke on it? (My eighth-grade gym teacher would have a heart attack!)
- ❖ Why are the shorts of professional basketball players so long? Rip Hamilton recently had a wardrobe malfunction during a game and changed his shorts on court. The sports commentator noted that players wear a lot of underclothing—I ask, why even bother wearing the shorts?
- ❖ I recently received some literature in the mail about the proper way to fly the American flag. It stated that the stars should always be to the north when hung vertically on east/west streets and to the east on north/south streets. Well what about on airplanes? The stars are

always to the right on the outside of airplanes regardless of how you face them, yet the flags always appear to be backward. Do the flags appear to be backward to me because I'm right-handed? Would a left-handed person see this issue differently than I? Also, who made up these rules, and what was their logic?

❖ Why is it that my cats want to sit on my lap just when I'm ready to stand up or when I'm ready to sit down?

❖ Why can't people purr like cats?

❖ Why do German shepherds shed so much?

❖ Is it, "I feel nauseous," or, "I feel nauseated?"

❖ Why are there wrinkles on my left earlobe but not on my right?

Advice to Myself When I'm Eighty Years Old

August 25, 2005

Dear Nicky,

I am writing this letter to you when I am forty-seven years old, and I'm wondering if you will still be referring to yourself as Nicky. This was the nickname given to you by your family of origin—actually by your mother who extracted the "Nic" from Monica. You used your nickname exclusively throughout high school and college, but, once you graduated, thought it time to return to your first name, which sounded more professional. I wonder if you will be referring to yourself as Monica when you are eighty—*Nicky* sounds too childish—and if you are not referring to yourself as Nicky, how does it feel to be addressed by that name in this letter? Does it bring back memories, and if so, are they good memories? What is the first picture that is conjured up in your mind when you hear the name *Nicky*?

Well, whatever name you go by at this stage in your life, I hope that you are happy. You know, you deserve to be happy. Yes, I don't have to remind you; you learned that lesson a long time ago. You deserve to be happy.

I am writing to you today because I am worried. I am worried about your happiness in the future, actually your present. I want you to be at peace with yourself, and I want others to be at peace with you too. I want people to look forward to spending time with you, not dread the visit or count down the minutes before they leave. I don't want you to say one day, as Grandma said to you, "No one has visited me in two days."

I am reminded of the game, Chicken Noodle Soup for the Kid's Soul. One day, I was playing this game with a boy at work, and the question he had to answer related to completing a kind gesture for someone who was geriatric. He asked me what geriatric meant. I told him that it was someone who was much older than he was—he was about eleven years old. His response was, "I could bring in an apple for my teacher." Good answer, however, his teacher was only twenty-five years old! You were over twenty-five years old then, and you're much older than twenty-five now. My wish for you is that people do nice things for you even without being asked.

I am writing this on the eve of Mom's eightieth birthday. Both Mom and Dad are still alive, and I am beginning to see characteristics in them that I saw in Grandma. This worries me. Is it inevitable that people do not grow old gracefully? Is it inevitable that I will not grow old gracefully?

The answer is *no*. You will grow old gracefully, and here are some reminders to help you along during this wonderful stage in your life:

1. Hygiene: Wash every day, in every nook and cranny. If you can't reach some places, get help. If you don't attend to these places, you will begin to smell; even if you can't smell the odor yourself, it is inevitable that these places will smell. Your senses will begin to deteriorate, this is a given. Just because you can't smell the odor doesn't mean you don't have an odor, and don't try to mask it with perfumes. Perfumes will not solve the problem. You need to wash. This goes for your teeth too. Your teeth, or dentures, need to be brushed every day!

2. Physical Health: Make sure you take your supplements, and whatever medication you are on, as directed by your physician. Your medication will not work if you only take it sporadically, and this will only make matters worse. Also, if you are feeling poorly, tell someone. Your loved ones won't know how you feel unless you tell them, and the sooner the better. Don't wait until the last minute to tell someone that you feel ill. Others have lives too and need time to free their schedules up to take you to the doctor. It's perfectly normal to ask for help, just make sure you ask for it at the right time. Others will begin to feel frustrated with you if you don't ask for help appropriately. Also, if you've received treatment and it hasn't worked, make certain that you tell someone. Remember when Mom had her stroke? You were driving her home when she admitted that she was still feeling odd. She ended right back in the hospital that evening. Even

if you are homesick, it is best to be truthful about your physical health for several reasons—to ensure that you get the appropriate care and that the problem is resolved, so that another crisis is not created, so that your loved ones are not burdened with the logistics of seeking care for you, and so that both you and your loved ones don't have to be burdened with extra worry. Also, if you cannot drive anymore, please let someone know. I don't know where you will be living when you are eighty—hopefully, transportation will not be an issue—but if it is, please don't deny it. If you can't drive and you ignore this situation, you are taking many people's lives into your own hands. Don't take unnecessary risks! A solution will be available—somehow, somewhere—so that you can remain independent for as long as possible. Also, try to eat balanced meals. I know that this has been a problem for you all your life—you have a tendency to stress eat—but the more balanced you eat, the better you will feel. Exercise is important too. You probably won't be completing any marathons anymore, so how are you planning on using your muscles? Walk every day if you can. If you can't, do armchair aerobics. Do something, anything to get your body moving!

3. Mental Health: Treat everyone you meet with kindness. Don't criticize others. Remember that every person you meet has their own history—don't judge them for it. Try not to take your frustrations out on others even if you're feeling grumpy—this will just alienate you. Meditate every day. If you can't remember your mantra, make one up! You have seen great progress with meditation—it calms you, assists you in remaining levelheaded, and helps you sleep better—keep it up. Be grateful for the small things as well as the large. Continue to pursue your passions. Draw, play piano, write, and sing every day! If your hands can't tolerate the movement anymore, be creative—try drawing with your mouth. So what if your creations don't look realistic—just get colors down on paper and emote. If you don't have a piano or keyboard available to you, make sure that you sing, sing, sing . . . and laugh, laugh, laugh! Don't forget your sense of humor. Be certain to find the humor in every situation. Although it may take a while, the humor will be there! Don't dwell on the past and especially negative situations. Think happy thoughts. Remember that you will always be provided for. Keep a journal, either written or on tape. Play games even if you don't have a partner. Play against yourself. Backgammon and Scrabble are always fun! And don't forget to read. Always find ways to remain mentally stimulated. Find a cause and volunteer. When in the company of others, don't interrupt. Try

to stay involved with the conversation. If you can't hear, let others know. People tend to become irritated when you suddenly interrupt and talk about something irrelevant. If you can't keep up with the conversation, if you are not verse with the topic, ask questions. Show others that you are interested in what they have to say. If you are completely baffled by the topic, remember to use your sense of humor then ask to change the topic to something less challenging. Invite other people over for coffee, or go out to eat if you can. Don't wait for others to invite you out. You don't need a special occasion to have contact with other people.

4. Pets: Pets are wonderful companions, but they need to be taken care of! This is a very difficult subject for me to address, especially since I'm writing this only four months after Alex's death. Even though you love dogs, please don't obtain one if you can't take care of it. Dogs need to be fed, exercised, and taken to the vet. As they age, they develop special needs too. If you can't provide the care, ask for help. If no one can help you, please consider giving the dog to someone who can—I know that this will be an extremely difficult task for you to do, but it's the best for the dog. If you can't provide the care, the dog suffers and you too. Cats are easier to care for, but be certain that you change their litter box. Don't take on any added obligations that you can't follow through with.

5. Politics: Vote! Your opinion counts. Help the public remember that the elderly have voices, too. Don't give up! Your issues are just as valid as the younger generations' issues are.

I think that's all for now. Life can be complicated at times, so I hope that this letter is helpful in meeting your needs. If I've forgotten anything, maybe you could write me back and let me know. I want the best for you.

Love,
Nicky

Epilogue

I cannot end this book without saying a word about Detroit. I love Detroit, and frankly, I don't understand why it was recently touted as being the most dangerous city in the nation. All major cities have crime and poverty. I know, I know. Two of my stories shed a bad light on Detroit, but both stories could have happened in any major city.

Detroit has a lot to offer. Here are just a few examples:

- ❖ The Detroit Institute of Arts
- ❖ The Detroit Film Theater
- ❖ The Detroit Science Center
- ❖ The Charles Wright African American Museum
- ❖ The Detroit Historical Museum
- ❖ The Fox Theater
- ❖ The Fischer Theater
- ❖ The Max M. Fisher Music Center
- ❖ The Detroit Opera House
- ❖ The Comerica Park
- ❖ The Ford Field
- ❖ The Joe (Louis Arena)
- ❖ The Hart Plaza
- ❖ The RiverWalk
- ❖ The Greektown
- ❖ The Mexicantown
- ❖ The Hockeytown Cafe
- ❖ The Whitney
- ❖ The Harmonie Park
- ❖ The Campus Martius

- ❖ The Detroit International Auto Show
- ❖ The Detroit-Windsor Freedom Festival
- ❖ The Detroit Free Press/Flagstar Bank Marathon

The list goes on and on.

There is always something to do in Detroit, so stop picking on us and come check us out!

Printed in the United States
128054LV00011B/224/P

9 781436 366076